INFANT/TODDLER LEARNING & DEVELOPMENT
PROGRAM GUIDELINES

Publishing Information

The *Infant/Toddler Learning and Development Program Guidelines* was developed by the Child Development Division, California Department of Education. It was edited by Faye Ong, working in cooperation with Mary Smithberger, Consultant, Child Development Division. It was prepared for printing by the staff of CDE Press: the cover and interior design were created and prepared by Juan Sanchez; typesetting was done by Jeannette Reyes. It was published by the Department, 1430 N Street, Sacramento, CA 95814-5901. It was distributed under the provisions of the Library Distribution Act and *Government Code* Section 11096.

ISBN 978-0-8011-1619-3

Ordering Information

Copies of this publication are available for $19.95 each, plus shipping and handling charges. California residents are charged sales tax. Orders may be sent to the California Department of Education, CDE Press, Sales Office, 1430 N Street, Suite 3207, Sacramento, CA 95814-5901; FAX (916) 323-0823. See page 156 for complete information on payment, including credit card purchases, and an order blank. Prices on all publications are subject to change.

A list of infant/toddler caregiving materials available for purchase may be found on pages 151–156. In addition, an illustrated *Educational Resources Catalog* describing publications, videos, and other instructional media available from the Department can be obtained without charge by writing to the address given above or by calling the Sales Office at (916) 445-1260.

Notice

The guidance in *Infant/Toddler Learning and Development Program Guidelines* is not binding on local educational agencies or other entities. Except for the statutes, regulations, and court decisions that are referenced herein, the document is exemplary, and compliance with it is not mandatory. (See *Education Code* Section 33308.5.)

Contents

A Message from the State Superintendent of Public Instruction

One of the most important ways we can support families of infants and toddlers is to provide high-quality child care and development programs that foster their children's optimal development. The first three years is a crucial time of life. To promote the kind of experiences young children need to prosper, the California Department of Education has created *Infant/Toddler Learning and Development Program Guidelines*.

Young children turn to adults for emotional security and for opportunities to learn. Infants and toddlers need care and education and close, nurturing relationships that provide them with a secure base for exploration, learning, and discovery. We know that the experiences we offer infants and toddlers have a lasting impact on their future success.

Research on brain development indicates that the brains of infants and toddlers are twice as active as those of adults. By the time children reach the age of three, they have become competent in at least one language, formed a sense of self, and learned about basic concepts such as cause-and-effect and quantity. Exploring books, being read to, listening to stories, and learning songs and rhymes set children on a path for literacy.

More than half of California's infants and toddlers receive care in child care centers, in family child care homes, and with relatives or neighbors outside the home. Research shows that good care and education contribute to children's social–emotional, intellectual, language, and motor development. High-quality programs work closely with family members and provide their children with environments, materials, and relationships that enrich learning and development. This document presents a comprehensive set of guidelines for care and education during the first three years of a child's life. It also identifies specific policies and practices for early childhood professionals to follow as they seek to create high-quality programs for infants and toddlers.

This document, *Infant/Toddler Learning and Development Program Guidelines*, complements California's *Prekindergarten Learning and Development Guidelines*. Together, these documents offer a coherent framework for extending the benefits of high-quality care and education to all young children.

No endeavor is as significant as the work of early childhood professionals. They have a direct and lasting impact on the lives of young children and families. With this document, we are seeking to provide leadership to the field and ensure that the impact of infant/toddler programs is a positive one. I hope that the *Infant/Toddler Learning and Development Program Guidelines* will help everyone to provide the very best care and education for our young children. The benefits of starting out life on a path to success will extend to communities and our state, for our children's future is our future.

JACK O'CONNELL
State Superintendent of Public Instruction

Acknowledgments

The creation of this guide involved many people. They included (1) a national panel of experts in early childhood development and early care and education; (2) a writing and development team from WestEd's Center for Child and Family Studies in Sausalito, California; (3) staff from the California Department of Education/Child Development Division; and (4) specialized groups of reviewers who provided feedback on important topics.

The expert panel members represent both academic and practical perspectives on all subjects addressed in the *Infant/Toddler Learning and Development Program Guidelines.* The guidelines and rationales in this guide were generated by the expert panel during three meetings from September 2002 through May 2003. Each panel member and his or her affiliation are listed below:

Carol Brunson Day, *President/CEO*
Council for Professional Recognition
Washington, D.C.

Richard M. Clifford, *Senior Scientist*
FPG Child Development Institute
University of North Carolina at Chapel Hill
Chapel Hill, North Carolina

Renatta Cooper, *Director*
Jones/Prescott Institute
Hixon Center for Early Childhood Education at Pacific Oaks College
Pasadena, California

Amy Laura Dombro, *Author/Consultant*
New York City, New York

Senta Greene, *CEO and Lead Consultant*
Full Circle: A Professional Consulting Agency
Stevenson Ranch, California

Stanley Greenspan, *Clinical Professor*
Psychiatry, Behavioral Sciences, and Pediatrics
George Washington University Medical School
Washington, D.C.

Janet Gonzalez-Mena, *Early Childhood Consultant*
WestEd Faculty
Program for Infant/Toddler Caregivers
Fairfield, California

Claire Lerner, *Codirector of Parent Education*
Zero to Three
Washington, D.C.

Alicia F. Lieberman, *Professor*
Department of Psychiatry
University of California, San Francisco
Director, Child Trauma Research Project
San Francisco General Hospital

Mary Jane Maguire Fong, *Professor*
Early Childhood Education
American River College
Sacramento, California

Oletha Murry, *Coordinator*
Community Child Development
Family Resource and Referral
Stockton, California

Alice Nakahata, *Instructor*
City College of San Francisco
Child Development & Family Studies Department
San Francisco, California

Dolores Norton, *Samuel Deutsch Professor*
School of Social Service Administration
University of Chicago
Chicago, Illinois

Note: The titles and affiliations of all individuals on this list were current at the time the guidelines were developed.

Jeree Pawl, *Director/Clinical Professor (Retired)*
Infant-Parent Program
University of California, San Francisco

Margie Perez-Sesser, *Instructor*
Child Development
Modesto Junior College
Modesto, California

Norma Quan Ong, *Early Childhood Educator*
San Francisco, California

Intisar Shareef, *Department Chairperson*
Early Childhood Education
Contra Costa College
Richmond, California

Louis Torelli, *Infant/Toddler Specialist Cofounder*
Spaces for Children
Berkeley, California

WestEd Faculty
Program for Infant/Toddler Caregivers
Sausalito, California

Yolanda Torres, *WestEd Faculty (Retired)*
Program for Infant and Toddler Caregivers
Pasadena, California

Norman Yee, *Commissioner*
San Francisco First Five Commission
San Francisco, California

Edward Zigler, *Sterling Professor of Psychology (Emeritus)*
Yale University Center in Child Development and Social Policy
New Haven, Connecticut

WestEd, Center for Child and Family Studies staff writers:
Peter Mangione, *Program Codirector*
Ron Lally, *Program Codirector*
Deborah Greenwald, *Project Director*
Sara Webb, *Program Associate*

California Department of Education
Sue Stickel, *Deputy Superintendent*
Curriculum and Instruction Branch
Michael Jett, *Director,* Child Development Division
Gwen Stephens, *Assistant Director,* Child Development Division

Mary Smithberger, *Child Development Consultant,* Child Development Division
Juanita Weber, *Child Development Consultant,* California School Age Families Education Program (Cal-SAFE)

Additional Contributors:
Joan Weaver, *Editing Consultant*
Rima Shore, *Consultant*

California Institute on Human Services, Sonoma State University
Anne Kuschner, *Project Director*
Linda Brault, *Project Director,* Beginning Together
Joanne Knapp-Philo, *Project Director,* StoryQUEST
Lara Jolin, *Technical Assistance Specialist*

Diane Harkins, *Program Director*
Family Child Care at Its Best, University of California Davis Extension

Susan Muenchow, *Senior Research Scientist*
American Institutes for Research

We thank the following programs for permitting photographs to be taken of the staff, children, and families:

5th Avenue Early Head Start
San Rafael, California

Andrea Schieb's Family Child Care
Livermore, California

The Associated Students Early Childhood Education Center at San Francisco State University
San Francisco, California

Cabrillo College Children's Center
Aptos, California

Citrus Community College
Glendora, California

Diablo Valley Montessori School
Lafayette, California

Fernald Child Study Center, University of California, Los Angeles
Los Angeles, California

Lana Carter's Family Child Care
Santa Rosa, California

Megan E. Daly Infant Development Program,
    University of California, Los Angeles
    Los Angeles, California

Olga King's Family Child Care
    Santa Rosa, California

Pacific Oaks Infant/Toddler/Parent Program
    Pasadena, California

Pasadena City College Child Development
    Center
    Pasadena, California

PG&E Children's Center
    San Francisco, California

Pilgrim Hill Early Head Start
    San Rafael, California

Photography:
    Keith Gaudet
    Sheila Signer
    Sara Webb

Part One: Background

Introduction

This publication, *Infant/Toddler Learning and Development Program Guidelines*, presents information about how to provide high-quality early care and education, including recommendations for program policies and day-to-day practices that will improve program services to *all*[1] infants and toddlers (children from birth to thirty-six months of age). It contains vitally important information about early learning and development. With this publication the California Department of Education intends to provide a starting point for strengthening all programs that educate and care for infants and toddlers, including centers, family child care homes, and kith and kin care. The guidelines specifically address the concerns of program leaders, teachers, and family members. They also inform community organizations, policymakers, business leaders, and others interested in improving the care and education of California's youngest children.

The guidelines pay particular attention to the role of the family in early care and education, to the inclusion of children with disabilities or other special needs, and to collaboration between programs and families. Because high-quality programming cannot be attained without attention to these topics in all components of care, the topics are woven throughout the publication rather than treated separately. In addition, family child care and care by relatives are included in the main body of the guidelines and, when necessary for clarity, are addressed individually.

How great is the need for high-quality care?

Large numbers of infants all over the nation are spending long hours in early care and education settings, many of which are of poor quality. California reflects a national trend, suffering from a scarcity of both the quantity and the quality of infant/toddler programs. Over half (58 percent) of California's infants and toddlers spend time in nonparental care. A quarter of them (26 percent) are in full-time care, defined as 35 or more hours per week (Snyder and Adams 2001). The demand for high-quality care overwhelms supply. This need is especially pronounced in low-income communities (Fuller and Holloway 2001), where few high-quality settings can be found. Statewide, only an estimated 5 percent of available spaces in licensed centers are for infant care (*California Child Care Portfolio* 2001).

The guidelines aim to increase the quality of programs that currently exist and provide a framework for the development of new high-quality programs. Increasing the number of high-quality settings will lead to a wide range

---

[1] Whenever infants, toddlers, or children are mentioned in this publication, the intention is to refer to all children. In some places the word *all* is used to emphasize the inclusive perspective presented in this publication.

of benefits, including enhancing school readiness, offering safe havens from abuse and neglect, and providing appropriate services for children with disabilities or other special needs.

What does quality look like in an infant/toddler program?

Infants and toddlers thrive in places where they can feel secure, express their drive to learn, and build their competence. They rely on adults for nurturance and guidance as they learn. When infants and toddlers receive care in a relationship that consistently meets their physical and emotional needs, that relationship becomes a base for exploration and discovery. They learn from being in close relationships in many different ways during the first three years of life. For example:

- A three-month-old infant who is hungry or tired counts on a caring adult to read her cues and meet her needs.
- A teacher repeats a song or finger play after a six-month-old looks into her eyes and coos, as if asking her to keep the experience going.
- A teacher, noticing the interest of a thirteen-month-old who is pointing at a picture in a book, labels the picture for the child.
- A fifteen-month-old finds himself in a safe and interesting environment that has been organized by his caregiver, who is attuned to his developmental capabilities.
- A twenty-two-month-old with asthma and her family come to feel assured by the treatment of her teacher, who knows how to give medication and communicates regularly with the family about the child's special health needs.
- A two-year-old whose family's primary language is different from the teacher's feels comforted when the teacher says one or two familiar words to her in her family's language.
- A thirty-month-old, feeling frustrated or angry, learns that she can trust her teacher to help her with difficult feelings.

What program policies, practices, and professional development activities lead to high quality?

Program policies and practices that support the development of positive relationships—in particular, relationships between teachers and families and teachers and children—provide the foundation for high-quality care and education. Some examples of policies and practices are as follows:

- Primary care
- Small groups
- Continuity of caregiving relationships
- Safe, interesting, and developmentally engaging environments and materials
- Inclusion of children with disabilities or other special needs
- Curriculum that is responsive to individual children's interests, needs, and developmental abilities

The professional development of teachers also enhances program quality. Teachers develop professionally through education, study, experience, and ongoing communication with children's families. Professional development can lead to changes in teachers' perspectives and approaches in such ways as the following:

- Teachers learn how to be responsive to young children and to support their learning and development.

3

- Teachers learn the importance of being emotionally available to young children and their families and of interacting in sensitive, predictable ways.
- Teachers learn how to respond to individual interests, strengths, family experiences, and approaches to learning.

What does research say about the components and the importance of quality?

In the last two decades, many studies have identified the benefits of good-quality care for young children. A large-scale national study conducted by the National Institute of Child Health and Human Development (NICHD 1997) looked at home-based and center-based care. The NICHD researchers observed more than 600 nonmaternal child care settings of all kinds: grandparents, in-home care, child care homes, and centers. The NICHD study documented that safe, clean, stimulating environments with small groups and low adult-to-child ratios were correlated with sensitive, responsive, and cognitively stimulating care. The research team reported that this higher quality of care, which included more positive language stimulation and interaction between the child and teacher, was positively related to the child's (1) language abilities at fifteen, twenty-four, and thirty-six months of age; (2) cognitive development at age two; and (3) eventual school readiness (NICHD 2000).

Another large-scale study, the *Cost, Quality, and Outcomes Study* (1995), looked at nearly 400 child care centers in four states, including California. The researchers found that children who attended higher-quality child care centers had higher cognitive (for example, math and language abilities) and social skills (for example, better peer relations and fewer behavior problems) in early elementary school (Peisner-Feinberg and others 1999a).

Although dedicated teachers try to do what is good for children, unfortunately, researchers have also found that many families with children under the age of thirty-six months do not have access to good or excellent care. Less than 10 percent of the centers that were originally studied in the *Cost, Quality, and Outcomes Study* (Peisner-Feinberg and others 1999b), including California programs, were judged to be of high quality. Rather than benefiting from early care, young children are often adversely affected by groups that are too big, by undesirable adult-to-child ratios, by teachers with little training, and by programs with low teacher pay and high teacher turnover.

What are the long-range benefits of high-quality programs?

James J. Heckman, a Nobel laureate in economic sciences, analyzed the impact of early experience on a person's later success and concluded that society should invest in the very young. He states (2000, 3):

Learning starts in infancy, long before formal education begins, and continues throughout life. . . . Significantly, this is a time when human ability and motivation are shaped by families and non-institutional environments. Early learning begets later learning and early success breeds later success, just as early failure breeds later failure. Success or failure at this stage lays the foundation for success or failure in school, which in turn leads to success or failure in post-learning.

Heckman goes on to say that when one considers the long-term economic benefits of having a society of self-confident, motivated learners, no other period in life is more important.

Guided by research, practice, and the advice of experts, this publication identifies policies and practices that beget early learning and development and pave the way for later success. Making an investment in infants, toddlers, and families means making an investment to support the preparation, continuing professional development, and appropriate compensation of infant care teachers.

Do infants and toddlers need teaching or caring?

Adults who care for infants and toddlers spend every moment both teaching and caring.[2] In centers and family child care homes, early childhood professionals are simultaneously caregivers and teachers, as their work affects infants' health, safety, development, and learning. They attentively care for a child's well-being as they discover ways to support the individual child's curiosity and exploration. What to name this complex role is a challenge. This publication uses the term *infant care teacher* to emphasize the comprehensive nature of providing care and facilitating learning and development. Infant care teachers treat caregiving routines as learning opportunities for the infant and set the stage for learning by providing developmentally appropriate, safe, inclusive, and engaging learning environments. They also introduce materials, make comments, offer suggestions, and ask questions of children based on observation and study of the children's learning and development.

How are the infant/toddler guidelines linked to the CDE's Desired Results system?

As stated earlier, the purpose of the guidelines is to help programs improve the quality of the early care and education they provide. Improved quality in turn should lead to better outcomes for infants, toddlers, and their families. Progress in implementing these guidelines is tracked and the outcomes of program improvement are documented through the California Department of

Education's comprehensive assessment system called Desired Results for Children and Families. This system defines four general goals for children, including those with disabilities or other special needs, and two goals for families:

1. Children are personally and socially competent.
2. Children are effective learners.
3. Children show physical and motor competencies.
4. Children are safe and healthy.
5. Families support their children's learning and development.
6. Families achieve their goals.

The Desired Results system consists of three components. Children's developmental progress is first assessed through the California Department of Education's Desired Results Developmental Profile-Revised (DRDP-R). These profiles address the first four Desired Results for children and give a comprehensive picture of individual children's learning and development. The DRDP-R provides a profile of each child across indicators such as self-concept, self-regulation, social interaction skills, language development, preliteracy knowledge and skills, cognitive development and problem solving, premathematics knowledge and skills, motor development, and awareness of health and safety. Then the program's progress in meeting goals for families is assessed through a family interview form. A program gains insights from information reported by families on how well it is helping families support their children and achieve their goals. The third component of the Desired Results system focuses on program quality. Depending on the type of setting it is, a program periodically uses the Infant/Toddler Environment Rating Scale, the Early Childhood Environment Rating Scale, or the Family Day Care Rating Scale to assess its quality.

> **Teaching and Caring Occur Together from the Beginning of Life**
>
> Infants learn the rhythms of speech, gestures, social rules, and the meaning of facial expressions from adults during the first months of life. Every moment in which an adult provides care to a young infant is a moment rich with learning. Above all, young infants learn how people respond to their communication and behavior. For example, when an adult responds to a young infant who is crying because of hunger, the infant not only experiences the satisfaction of being fed but also learns that his crying will bring a response from an adult.

---

[2] The word *adult* is used to describe the role of the adult, including a teenage parent who has taken on adult responsibilities as a parent.

In addition to informing programs on how well they are implementing the guidelines, the Desired Results system is an integral part of facilitating the learning and development of infants and toddlers. Programs use the DRDP-R to plan learning environments and experiences that fit children's current level of development and provide an appropriate amount of challenge. Because the infant/toddler guidelines and Desired Results system work hand in hand, the link between them will be referenced throughout this publication.

How do the infant/toddler guidelines relate to the prekindergarten guidelines?

This publication is a companion to the *Prekindergarten Learning and Development Guidelines* published by the California Department of Education in 2000. The prekindergarten guidelines describe high-quality programming for preschools and make recommendations for curriculum and practice. The infant/toddler guidelines resemble the format and approach of the prekindergarten guidelines. The infant/toddler guidelines were developed to link to the prekindergarten guidelines and focus on experiences that help young children make the transition to preschool programs.

Although the overall approach of the two publications is similar, they are distinct due to differences between the two age groups. For example, this publication places the family at the center of programs for infants and toddlers since early development unfolds in the context of the family. By building a relationship with the family, infant/toddler programs take the first step in facilitating the child's learning and development. In addition, because much of what children learn in the first months and years of life occurs during caregiving routines (greetings and departures, diaper changing, feeding, napping), the infant/toddler guidelines pay close attention to everyday routine interactions. Preschool-age children still have much to learn about themselves, but they have already established a basic sense of identity. In contrast, identity formation is just starting for infants and toddlers. Their emerging sense of self, sense of belonging, and sense of confidence are intimately connected to their family and culture. The messages family members convey during interactions profoundly influence how infants and toddlers feel about themselves and what they expect from relationships with adults and children. Finally, this publication necessarily places greater emphasis on health and safety considerations than do the prekindergarten guidelines. Because infants' immune systems are still developing and they are beginning to learn to move their bodies, both the caregiving routines and the physical environment require special attention.

What do the infant/toddler guidelines offer?

The *Infant/Toddler Learning and Development Program Guidelines* is based on the field's current understanding of young children during the first three years of life. Designed to encourage continuous improvement of programs, the guidelines offer a blueprint for early care and education. They focus on several areas:

- *Research-based practice.* This publication summarizes research findings that can guide day-to-day decisions and practices when combined with information from the children's families, from teachers'

experience and education, and from specialists supporting individual children.

- *Relationships and experience.* The guidelines place relationships at the center of healthy learning and development. Each relationship—between child and teacher, the family and teacher, staff members and administration, and staff members and specialists supporting individual children and families—helps programs provide high-quality early care and education.

- *Alignment of curriculum with children's learning and development.* In the guidelines, curriculum is defined as a process. Teachers observe children, document their observations, assess children's developmental progress, reflect on their observations and assessments, discuss them with colleagues, and plan and introduce learning experiences based on this process. By respecting children as active participants in learning, teachers create an environment of experiences that fit each child's evolving interests and abilities. The DRDP-R works hand in hand with this publication, offering a framework to teachers as they align curriculum with children's learning and development.

- *Professional development, reflective supervision, and reflective practice.* The guidelines provide direction for ongoing professional development of teachers. An important part of professional development occurs when teachers reflect upon, or think about, day-to-day experiences with children and families as well as spend time with supervisors reflecting on practice. Research indicates that having well-prepared staff is one of the key components of high-quality care and education. In settings with well-prepared teachers, all infants and toddlers have a wider range of language experiences, engage in more complex play with objects, and are more creative in solving problems and making discoveries (Howes 1997).

- *Context.* The guidelines take into account the impact of context on learning and development. A young child's life is influenced by everything—from the expression on a teacher's face to neighborhood sounds at night. Every moment of a child's life is a learning experience. The context for learning and development includes the social, emotional, and physical world in which a child lives—all of which influence a child's daily experience in care and education, a family's participation in the program, and a teacher's ability to respond sensitively to a child's strengths, needs, and interests.

How is this publication organized?

Part One summarizes the research and ideas supporting these guidelines. Four chapters make up Part One:

- Chapter 1 focuses on building relationships with families. This chapter describes how all infants and toddlers enter early

care and education programs as newly developing members of families and communities. Important throughout childhood, the family's involvement in the development and care of their child is intense during the infant/toddler years. This publication recognizes the family's fundamental role by emphasizing a family-oriented approach to the care and education of infants and toddlers.

- Chapter 2 summarizes current research on early development, including brain development, that has shed new light on how to nurture infants and toddlers.

- Chapter 3 defines the role of the teacher. This chapter gives an overview of the teacher as a reflective practitioner who forms close, caring relationships with young children and their families and explores ways to facilitate their learning and development.

- Chapter 4 describes program leadership and administration. Program leadership and administration are essential in all settings—infant/toddler centers where a director often leads the program; a family child care home where the provider leads the program; or kith and kin care where the child's relative or neighbor is responsible for both facilitating learning and attending to administrative responsibilities.

Part Two, divided into two chapters, presents the guidelines. (See Appendix A for a summary of the guidelines.)

- Chapter 5 contains guidelines for operating an infant/toddler program, including developing relationship-based policies and practices and maintaining a safe and healthy environment.

- Chapter 6 describes the curriculum process of facilitating learning for infants and toddlers, including children with disabilities or other special needs. Teachers, program leaders, and family members share important roles in responding to infants as active and motivated learners.

Both chapters open with a brief introduction. Each section begins with a rationale explaining why the guideline is important. Action points or recommendations are given for applying the guidelines in diverse child care settings. Desired Results and, when applicable, indicators from the DRDP-R are also identified for each of the guidelines.

Part Three lists resources on which the guidelines are based. Resources consist of research publications, curricula for infants and toddlers, and lists of relevant organizations.

From beginning to end, this publication invites teachers and program leaders to forge relationships with families and, together with families, create high-quality experiences for all infants and toddlers. Such experiences not only benefit children and families during the first three years but also influence their development throughout their lives.

CHAPTER 1

The Development of Programs with Families

"Families and communities are the ground-level generators and preservers of values and ethical systems. Individuals acquire a sense of self not only from observation of their own bodies and knowledge of their own thoughts but from their continuous relationship to others, especially close familial or community relations, and from the culture of their native place, the things, the customs, the honored deeds of their elders."

—J. W. Gardner, *Building Community*

This chapter describes the crucial role of the family during the first three years of life and explains why, in order to achieve a high-quality program, infant care teachers begin by working together with families. The approach presented here places infant/toddler care in the context of families, rather than as a program separate from families. The chapter then considers the nature of relationships and communication with diverse families within a family-oriented approach to the care and education of infants and toddlers.

The Central Role of Families

Children are not islands. They are intimately connected with their families. In their relationships children and their families each have a significant influence on the other. The family adapts to the child, and the child to the family.[1]

The family's influence on the learning and development of an infant or toddler surpasses all other influences.

Family relationships have more influence on a child's learning and development than any other relationships he has. Family members know him better than anyone else. They know his usual way of approaching things, his interests, how he likes to interact, how he is comforted, and how he learns. Family members understand his strengths, and they have learned how to help him with any special needs he may have. Just as important, the child's relationships with family members shape the way he experiences relationships outside the home.

"What young children learn, how they react to events and people around them, and what they expect from themselves and others are deeply affected by their relationships with parents, the behavior of parents, and the environment of the homes in which they live" (*From Neurons to Neighborhoods* 2000, 226).

Infants and toddlers learn and develop in the context of their families' cultural communities.

Families are not islands; they are connected to cultural communities. Each family has beliefs, values, and expectations for their children that are rooted in cultural communities yet reflect the unique perspective of that family. Culture also influences families' perspectives and approaches to supporting children with disabilities or other special needs. Families often participate in more than one community, and no two families follow

cultural rules in exactly the same way. In fact, infants, toddlers, and their families develop within a set of "nested" communities, each one influencing the child's development and identity. These communities may include neighborhoods, towns, churches or temples, infant/toddler programs, and schools. Each community has its own culture, and each has an influence on the family and the child.

The following illustration is adapted from Bronfenbrenner (1979): Imagine the child's world to be represented by a series of concentric circles with the individual child at the center. Each circle represents a sphere of influence that affects the child's life. These spheres, which include family, child care, community, school, the media, the workplace, and government, to name but a few, are nested within one another, extended outward from the child herself.

Communities can be a source of strength for families and their children, providing support and resources. These resources can be services to people who make up the families' communities. For instance, neighbors in a community may provide friendship and emotional support to one another, celebrate family events, and help families cope with stress. A community may have available prenatal and health care, nutrition, and early intervention services—all of which help children as they develop. All infant/toddler programs represent a very important kind of supportive community for families and their young children. They are communities where infants and toddlers spend large amounts of time, learn, and develop significant relationships with adults and other children. For these communities to work well, families must be respected, have a sense of belonging, and be viewed as active participants.

When a very young child enters an infant/toddler program, both the infant and the infant's family experience dramatic changes in their lives. The infant is faced, usually for the first time, with the challenges of adapting to a strange environment, different routines, and new relationships. The family members, too, must make a difficult adjustment—the sharing of the care of their child with someone outside the family.

---

[1] The term "family member" is used throughout this publication to describe the people who are primarily responsible for a child, whether they are parents, grandparents, foster families, or others.

The Nature of Relationships Between Programs and Families

An infant/toddler program is a system of relationships (Rinaldi 2003). Within this system, the relationship between the family and the program is key to the program's relationship with the child. Through a welcoming relationship with the family, the child's teachers begin to understand the family's perspectives, strengths, needs, routines, hopes, and expectations. This understanding helps teachers to appreciate not only who the child is but also the child's experience of the world.

Within a system of relationships, the relationship between the family and the infant care teacher is key. For a family, the experience of entering an infant/toddler setting may be highly emotional. Family members usually have anxiety about the separation from their child and may feel ambivalent about leaving their child. For many families these feelings and experiences can often be intensified when their child has a disability or other special need. All families feel protective of their child and want the best for her. Their beliefs about what is right for their child reflect both their culturally based expectations and their unique relationship experiences with her. They are often unsure what to expect from the infant/toddler program or what kind of relationship they will have with it.

The Importance of Establishing Working Relationships

Both families and teachers feel the strong impulse to protect infants and toddlers. Teachers can be more responsive to family members' strong emotions if they have established a positive relationship based on two-way communication. When a family member and a teacher have different beliefs about how to nurture a child, each may react emotionally. Being responsive to family interests early in the relationship helps build trust. In programs based on relationships with families, teachers seek and value the family's voice as the best source of information about the child (such as her temperament, strengths, interests, or needs). Family members often enjoy talking to someone who knows and appreciates their child's unique personality and sense of humor. This connection between families and teachers can be one of joy and

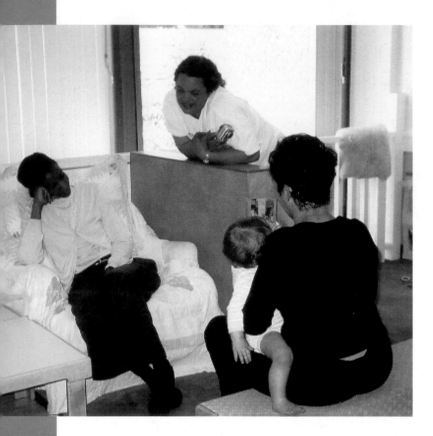

humor as they share stories about children's activities at home and in care. When concerns do arise, the existing relationship provides a natural transition for conversing about them. The family member and the teacher know each other and have already developed some trust.

Cultural Perspectives on Nurturing Young Children

Williams and De Gaetano (1985) describe culture as a way of life of a group of people, including shared views of the world and social realities, values and beliefs, roles and relationships, and patterns or standards of behavior. Through culture children gain a sense of identity, a feeling of belonging, and beliefs about what is important in life, what is right and wrong, how to care for themselves and others, and what to celebrate, eat, and wear. When children are raised only in their home culture, they learn those lessons almost effortlessly. When they spend some of their formative years in child care with people who were not raised in their culture and who do not necessarily share the same family and community values, the learning of those important early lessons becomes more complex.

A person's approach to nurturing infants and toddlers reflects one's values. Certain values that are familiar may be experienced as "natural," whereas other values are considered "different." For example, the early childhood profession in the United States has historically emphasized that young children be set on a path toward independence and encouraged to care for themselves as early as possible. The common practice of encouraging older babies to feed themselves reflects the profession's emphasis on independence. Recently, however, an increasing number of early childhood professionals are recognizing the diversity of perspectives on independence. Many families whose children attend child care programs value interdependence more than independence. This value can be observed in the ways children are taught to help one another and to respect the needs of others (such as staying at the table until everyone is finished). Early care and education programs have begun to modify program practices and policies to weave the concept of interdependence as well as the concept of independence into the fabric of care.

Sometimes, differences of opinion surface between the infant care program and a family about how to care for children. Addressing these differences often provides opportunities for teachers to learn and grow together with families. Teachers need to initiate conversations with the family to find out the family members' thoughts about caring for the child. The family's perspectives and values may or may not reflect the cultural communities in which the family participates. Even when a family belongs to the same cultural community as the teacher, the teacher's perspective may differ from the family's, as each person interprets cultural rules and expectations differently. In a family child care home, the culture of the provider's family is strongly represented in various ways, such as its communication styles, artwork, child-rearing practices, and music. Home settings present an opportunity for providers to initiate discussions with family members about one another's cultures, values, and beliefs.

Open, respectful communication helps the teacher bridge children's experiences in the program with their experiences at home. When a teacher becomes aware of different beliefs, values, practices, or communication styles, open and respectful communication with the family is especially important. This type of communication means being thoughtful and willing to share one's own beliefs and values without imposing them on the family. It also means learning from family members what their beliefs and values are without judging them. Through conversations with the family, the teacher may discover ways she can adapt her practices so that the child's experiences in the infant/toddler setting closely connect with his experiences at home.

Conclusion

Every relationship in an infant/toddler program affects the well-being and development of the child. Teachers who understand the fundamental importance of the family–child relationship place a high priority on building a positive, reciprocal relationship with the family. They know that only the family can provide information on the child's unique relationship experiences at home.

Open, two-way communication between teachers and families enables them to learn from one another and to gain insights into how to facilitate the individual child's learning and development. Recent child development research, as described in the next chapter, sketches a picture of infants and toddlers as motivated learners who actively seek relationships with adults. The usefulness of insights from this research is greatly enhanced by information from the family, for it completes the picture of the individual child.

Resolving a Difference

In one infant/toddler center, babies would arrive with amulets and medicine bags hanging around their necks for health reasons. The center staff members decided to remove those items while the babies were at the center so the babies would not strangle. The staff members did not think the amulets served a purpose, anyway, but the parents felt strongly that they must remain on the babies all through the day. Finally, after much discussion, the parents and staff members managed to hear each other. Instead of forbidding the babies to arrive with little bags around their necks, they found ways to attach the bags to the babies' clothes so the bags would not present a potential strangling hazard and the babies could still have their preventive or curative amulets with them.

CHAPTER 2
New Insights into Early Learning and Development

All infants and toddlers are motivated to seek relationships and explore with curiosity and energy the world around them. From these powerful motivations, development proceeds and is integrated across the social–emotional, language, physical, and intellectual domains. Learning in different developmental domains often occurs at the same time, and young children may quickly shift their focus from one type of learning to another. All infants and toddlers continually seek to make discoveries and understand the world of people and things. They strive to learn to communicate and deepen their relationships with the adults who care for them. They also rely on those adults to keep them safe and help them develop a sense of physical and emotional security.

Two-year-old Graciela tries going down the slide by herself for the first time, and Jake races up after her. She remembers her teacher telling another child, "Use your words. Say, 'My turn.'" She then turns to Jake and says "My turn" as she scoots down the slide. At the bottom she sees a ball, and Jake cries out, "Mine!" She tries rolling the ball up the slide to him, but it simply rolls back down. They both find this funny, and it turns into a game, with Graciela rolling the ball up, and Jake trying to catch it before it rolls back. Their teacher watches and smiles, saying, "You're playing with the ball together! And look, the ball keeps rolling down!" Graciela has made some important discoveries about her ability to master her movement, her new way of using language, and her competence in handling new social situations while learning that objects do not roll uphill.

During the first three years of life, children constantly change as they move through three stages of development. From birth to eight or nine months of age, children form their first expectations about emotional security. From about eight months to sixteen or eighteen months of age, they use their emerging abilities to move and explore their environment. Older infants, eighteen to thirty-six months of age, express their developing identity through words such as "me," "mine," and "no" (*Developmentally Appropriate Practice* 1997; Lally and others 1995).

Although all children go through the major stages of infancy, no two children do it the same way. Each child is born with a unique combination of strengths, abilities, and temperament traits, along with an amazing potential to learn and develop. Research on early brain development has illuminated how biological potential and the child's environment combine to shape who the child is and the unique way she develops.

Four major insights have emerged from research on early learning and development:

- Infants and toddlers learn and develop in the context of important relationships.
- Infants and toddlers are competent.
- Infants and toddlers are vulnerable.
- Infants and toddlers are a unique blend of nature and nurture.

Learning about these four insights can help programs and infant care teachers facilitate young children's learning and development. This chapter summarizes recent research and offers ideas on how to use this information in early care and education programs.

Insight 1: Infants and toddlers learn and develop in the context of important relationships.

How infants develop rests on a genetic, biological unfolding and the experiences they have as that unfolding happens. Who this baby is and how he is perceived influences the care he receives. How responsive adults are to the particular baby determines what kinds of relationships are created. Are relationships joyful, mutual, awkward, in tune, erratic, or harmonious? Such experiences have an effect on who the child will be, including when he will learn and what he will be able to learn. Adults' perception of when the child is ready to explore and learn influences what adults do with the child, which in turn contributes to his understanding of himself. The best chance for this development to proceed well is if the care the child receives is sensitively responsive to the particular child he is—a child different from any other. The adult's awareness and understanding of this unique child contribute to the child's fundamental sense of possibility for himself, his competence, and his effectiveness—all of which will be part of his emerging sense of self.

"[W]hen young children and their caregivers are tuned in to each other, and when caregivers can read the child's emotional cues and respond appropriately to his or her needs in a timely fashion, their interactions tend to be successful and the relationship is likely to support healthy development in multiple domains, including communication, cognition, social-emotional competence, and moral understanding" (*From Neurons to Neighborhoods* 2000, 28).

Relationships, while important throughout life, play an especially crucial role in the early years.

A nurturing relationship with at least one loving, responsive adult is essential for a child to develop trust and a healthy sense of self. Within the child's first relationships he learns about himself, establishes a base to explore the world, and discovers how to engage adults to meet his needs.

Relationships support all learning domains.

When an infant feels safe, she can focus her attention on exploring and learning about her world. She starts to feel competent when adults provide experiences that capture her interest and provide the support she needs to master new skills. For example, a five-month-old learns that, through making sounds and actively moving her arms, legs, or other body parts, she can let her teacher know she wants to play peek-a-boo again—and her teacher responds by playing. When young children know that caring adults are physically and emotionally available to provide encouragement, help, love, and appreciation, a strong foundation is set for healthy relationships and lifelong learning.

Infants and toddlers also learn by developing relationships with one another. In the early months of life, infants learn by observing and imitating other children. As they grow older, they engage in similar play while imitating each other. By the time they are older infants, they play together; for example, building with blocks, helping each other solve problems, and taking on different roles in pretend play. Infants and toddlers become emotionally connected to one another. In their early relationships, they learn how it feels to be in a conflict, to resolve conflicts with other children, and to be comforted by another child as well as to comfort another child.

Self-regulation develops in the context of relationships.

One of the most important developments in the first three years of life is that infants and toddlers begin to learn to self-regulate. In other words, they are gaining control over their physical and emotional responses. When the adult responds predictably and positively, infants learn that after communicating a need it will be met promptly. They also learn that a caring adult can comfort and help them when emotions are overwhelming (Schore 1994). Consistent, prompt responses help infants feel secure as well as help them learn to wait and regulate their emotional responses even though they feel some stress. In fact, research has shown that secure early relationships can affect children's biochemistry, buffering them from the negative impact of stress (Gunnar 1999).

Secure Relationships Support Exploration

Jenna, who was born prematurely and has been delayed in developing language and motor skills, rolls toward the low shelf. She bangs the bowl she is holding on the hard surface of the shelf and looks expectantly at her infant care teacher, Josh. He smiles at her and says. "Hi, Jenna, I see you over there!" Jenna wiggles delightedly and holds the bowl out to him and squeals as she pulls it back close to her chest. "You are holding that bowl and showing it to me. You played with that same bowl yesterday, didn't you?" Josh moves closer and gently touches Jenna's arm. "See? You brought me close to you." Josh sits nearby while Jenna turns back to the shelf and finds another bowl to explore.

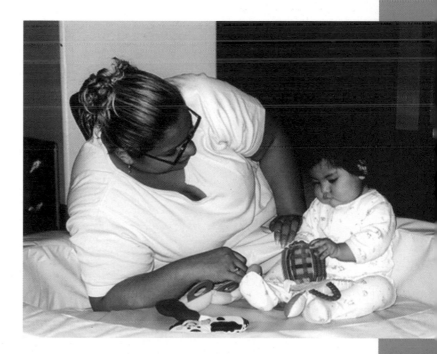

Early Experiences, Early Learning

Young children are always learning—even when the adults interacting with them are not aware that they are teaching. Think of the newborn who, when she cries out in the middle of the night, is gently picked up and cuddled, hears a soothing voice, and is gazed at lovingly as she is fed. Now think of another newborn who, when she cries out in the middle of the night, hears doors banging and angry voices, is picked up roughly, and then is fed, facing outward, in rigid arms. These two babies are learning very different things about the world.

What lessons are toddlers learning in the following examples? Mia is told not to grab toys from others as her caregiver angrily grabs the toy from her to give back to the other child. Mia continues to grab toys from other children and becomes angry herself. Aleisha sees her caregiver hand another child, James, his blanket when he cries as his father leaves. Then, the next day, as James stares out the window watching his father leave, Aleisha brings James his blanket to comfort him.

"Developing and maintaining the ability to notice and control primary urges such as hunger and sleep—as well as feelings of frustration, anger, and fear—is a lifelong process. Its roots begin with the external regulation provided by parents or significant caregivers, and its healthy growth depends on a child's experiences and the maturation of the brain" (Perry 1996, 2).

Eventually, children start to anticipate both their inner feelings and cues from other people that signal a stressful situation. Being able to anticipate stress, older infants plan and take action to cope with it. For example, when feeling tired, a child may look for her blanket and find a quiet place to rest.

The rhythm of playful social interaction—giving a message and then waiting for a response—helps children develop the ability to moderate impulsive action in order to engage socially. Adults who read young infants' cues and adapt to their rhythm and pace provide them with opportunities to practice self-regulation. The benefits of having an adult who adapts to one's rhythm and pace extends to all children, including children with disabilities or other special needs.

The ability to regulate socially develops hand in hand with the ability to maintain attention in various situations (Sroufe 1995). The child's daily experiences with an adult who pays attention to him strengthen his developing capacity to be attentive. From these experiences the child expands his inborn capacity to engage in focused exploration of the world of people and things.

Insight 2: Infants and toddlers are competent.

Infants and toddlers come into the world ready to love and eager to form social ties—they are born looking for us. In the first hours of life, babies respond to touch, snuggle up to their mothers' breasts, and gaze at their parents' faces. The way children are responded to provides their first information about this new world they are entering and how it feels.

All infants and toddlers, including those with disabilities or other special needs, are curious, active, self-motivated learners.

Babies begin to explore the world and the people around them from the moment they are born. A newborn's brain is wired at birth to begin paying attention to the things that will matter most to his development. On the first day of life, he stares longer at faces than at other objects. Within days he begins to anticipate feedings, voices, and smells. The inborn drive to learn continues and expands as the infant grows. A toddler who is given a set of nesting cups will begin to explore them without instructions from an adult—fitting them together, stacking them, trying to fit other objects in them, or banging them together to see what sounds they make. Infants and toddlers are active, motivated learners who have their own curriculum. Like scientists, they test out ways to explore and discover. They store new information away so they can use it again in their next experiment.

Infants and toddlers teach themselves when they are free to move on their own.

When free to do so, infants and toddlers move almost all the time. Very young infants move their limbs in and out as they gradually gain control of their muscles. They study their hands and watch intently as they begin to find ways to use them to grasp and stroke people or things within their reach. Infants relish the struggle of reaching, stretching, rolling, and lifting their bodies. They find new ways to touch and discover and take delight in their developing abilities to move. They gain information about the world through large- and small-muscle movement. For all young children, including those who have differences or delays in their movement skills, learning happens when they are moving. Some children will move constantly, with a high level of energy, while others will observe for awhile and start by moving slowly, sometimes tentatively. No matter what their styles of moving are, when infants and toddlers reach, crawl, climb, push heavy objects, fall, get up, and move on, they make new discoveries about the world around them and the capabilities of their bodies.

Communication and language begin developing early.

Communication and language development start earlier than many people realize (Kuhl 2000). In fact, babies hear language well before birth, and soon after birth they

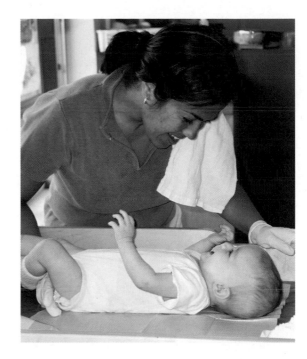

recognize the voices of family members and other familiar adults. Early in life, young infants engage in give-and-take communication by making sounds, facial expressions, and gestures when adults communicate verbally and nonverbally with them and give them time to respond. The first back-and-forth exchanges of sound and other nonverbal cues between a baby and an adult are like conversations—they follow

the same pattern. These early "conversations" lay the groundwork for children's developing language skills during early childhood, which, in turn, gives them a good start for learning to read at school age. Early "conversations" are richest when adults are responsive to infants' feelings and interests. As communication and language develop, so does cognition (Fernald 1993). Adults who sing, talk, ask questions, listen, and label things when interacting with young children directly affect how the children's brains develop (Shore 1997).

Sometimes, children learn one language at home and another in the infant/toddler program. Because infants usually have an easy time learning more than one language, they often begin to explore, understand, and speak both languages. At first children who learn two languages may mix them up, but if both languages are respected and supported, toddlers soon become competent at using both of them. However, if children are given the message that the language in the infant/toddler program is preferable to their language at home, they may stop learning their families' languages. In so doing, they may lose their ability to communicate with family members. Having teachers who are fluent in the child's home language is optimal. However, hearing even a few words of the home language spoken at the program not only supports learning in the family's language but also offers the comfort of familiar sounds in a new place. Continuing to learn the home language strengthens the child's developing sense of self. Families also appreciate that the program values their cultural experiences and languages.

Insight 3: Infants and toddlers are vulnerable.

Infants depend on adults for survival. Compared to other animals, human infants are helpless for a very long time (Hamburg 1996). Foals can stand up when they are born, and baby sea turtles take care of themselves from the moment they hatch. For human infants, their very survival—and well-being—hinges on the protection and care they receive from adults.

Infants orient to adults for protection and learning.

Young children orient to adults not only for protection but also to learn how to be a competent participant in their family. The challenge for adults is to protect and nurture infants while being respectful of their developing competence. Being responsive to both the vulnerable and the competent sides of an infant takes understanding and sensitivity. An important part of this dual role is attending to how one says and does things with infants and toddlers. During the first three years of life, children are forming their first impressions of the world. They are finding out how they feel in different situations and how others make them feel. The ways in which adults relate to them has a profound influence on their developing sense of security and their self-confidence.

Nurturance from adults affects the developing brain.

Recent research on brain development has added to knowledge about the infant's vulnerability. Early experiences with adults have a direct influence on the connective pathways that are formed in the brain during the early years (*From Neurons to Neighborhoods* 2000). In other words, experience alters the structure of the brain, which in turn affects the way the brain works. For example, researchers found that babies born prematurely grew at an unusually slow rate owing to chemical effects on their brains, despite having their physical needs met in the hospital. These babies, separated from their parents and isolated in incubators with minimal human contact, had high levels of cortisol—a major stress hormone that signals the body to shut down in order to survive. With an elevated level of cortisol, genetic activity slows so that cells cannot divide, which reduces the child's growth rate (Kuhn and others 1991). Other researchers reported that when babies born prematurely were touched—held, hugged, and gently massaged—their weight increased from 12–17 grams to 25 grams per day. Those children also were able to leave the hospital six days earlier than children born prematurely who did not receive touch therapy (Field and others 1986).

As stated earlier in this chapter, research shows infants come into the world with an inborn capacity to learn language. Usually they learn language quickly and easily. However, their incredible potential to learn language depends entirely on having opportunities to communicate with other humans. Within the typical range of infants' experiences with language, there are vast differences. Researchers found that, by age three, children whose family members spoke to them frequently had much larger vocabularies than children whose family members spoke less often to them (Hart and Risley 1995, 2003).

The idea that infants are both competent and vulnerable reflects the view that both nature and nurture contribute to development. Most scientists believe that the long-standing nature-versus-nurture debate is no longer relevant. Young children's development reflects not only the genetic potential and capacities they are born with but also the experiences they have. Development hinges on the interaction between nature *and* nurture.

All infants and toddlers, including children with disabilities or other special needs, are well equipped by nature to seek out close, caring relationships that give them the security they need to grow and learn.

From birth infants seek ways to feel safe. Infants come into the world equipped biologically with signals to elicit help from adults.

The cry is perhaps the most powerful but certainly not the only signal children give. The tender appearance of young infants draws a protective response in most adults. Infants' smiles and coos bring out warm responses and feelings of joy. To be responsive, adults rely on cues from infants to find out how best to respond to them. Adults come to understand when children are hungry, tired, ill, uncomfortable, or just fussy. Infants quickly learn to communicate to lessen their vulnerability. For example, infants learn that if they make a certain sound or movement adults will come to give them attention. Later, infants are able to go to adults. As infants and adults develop relationships, both of them create ways to ensure the infants' safety and well-being.

Infants rely on consistent, predictable, and positive experiences with adults to become secure.

One key to security for infants is being nurtured daily by a few people in predictable and consistent ways. A young infant feels confident when he recognizes the face and voice of the infant care teacher who greets him

in the morning. The adult also gets to know the infant's subtle cues and unique ways of communicating. Children who form secure attachments with adults over time, both at home and in an infant/toddler program, explore their world confidently and become increasingly competent in social situations.

Secure relationships matter over time. Researchers who have followed children over several years have found that securely attached babies and toddlers grow into more competent school-age children. As one researcher has said, "Confidence in the relationship . . . becomes self-confidence" (Sroufe 1995, p. 220). Research has shown that infants form attachments with their family members as well as their child care providers. Researchers say that infants who form secure attachments to their child care providers tend to be better able to adapt to new people and situations and master new social challenges. In addition, children who are securely attached to their providers show more competent interactions with adults and more advanced peer play, both during the child care years and on into the second grade (Howes 1999, 2000; *From Neurons to Neighborhoods* 2000). Secure relationships with child care providers support healthy social and emotional development. Benefits can be seen in other areas as well, including communication skills, intellectual development, and moral development (*From Neurons to Neighborhoods* 2000).

Infants' physical health and safety are in the hands of those who care for them.

Because their immune systems have not fully developed, infants and toddlers are more susceptible than older children to infectious disease. Generally, licensed infant/toddler settings are effective in safeguarding the health of young children. Yet despite improvements in recommended health care practices, many children in infant/toddler settings are exposed to serious illnesses in the early years. Awareness of children's special health concerns and appropriate action by infant/toddler programs based on those concerns are important preventive health measures. Programs can also be useful resources to families by maintaining contact with a health care provider or adviser. (Policies and practices that programs implement as preventive health strategies are described in Chapter 4.)

Because infants and toddlers constantly explore the environment and take risks to test their developing large motor abilities, accidental injury presents a danger to them. Today, more safety information is available about accidental injury than ever before, thanks to mandatory safety labeling, safety-oriented Web sites, and public service announcements. Infant/toddler programs can work together with families to safeguard children and help families gain access to information on child safety in their own language. In particular, programs can provide information about the importance of using appropriate infant or child seats in cars.

Infants with disabilities, other special needs, or vulnerabilities benefit from early intervention.

One of the most important messages to emerge from the last decade's early childhood research is the power of prevention and early intervention. Prevention is the first step in addressing young children's vulnerabilities. Because outside influences such as the environment and nurturing relationships are important for optimal brain development, high-quality infant/toddler programs may prevent some later difficulties through responsive and consistent care. Infant/toddler programs also contribute to the lasting impact of early intervention in many ways, beginning with identification (Erickson and Kurz-Riemer 1999). Disabilities or other special needs often become apparent in the first three years of life. Careful observation, ongoing communication with families, and developmental screening can lead to early identification and appropriate referral. In California the system of early intervention services for children from birth to three years of age is called California Early Start.

(See Appendix B for more information on California Early Start. The National Early Childhood Technical Assistance Center Web site [http://www.nectac.org] provides links to similar systems in other states.)

After a referral teachers can collaborate with families and early intervention specialists to ensure that children's learning and development are supported in all settings where they spend time (Carr and Hanson 2001).

Infants and toddlers, like all children, are vulnerable to abuse and neglect.

When family members are experiencing high levels of stress, programs can help them obtain services and resources. The help the family receives can reduce stress and lessen the likelihood of child neglect or abuse. In addition, program policies that support close relationships between a teacher and a small group of children allow the teacher to know individual children well and to readily identify signs of risk. In the unfortunate situation in which action must be taken to protect a child, a program must follow the state reporting laws. In California, county departments that administer local health and human services provide information on reporting suspected child abuse and neglect. (For immediate help, a national hotline [1-800-4 A CHILD] provides direct access to local agencies.)

Insight 4: Infants and toddlers are a unique blend of nature and nurture.

Each child is born with his own unique biological inheritance, learning style, abilities, rate of development, and ways of relating to others. The child's uniqueness reflects his experiences in relationships, genetic predisposition, and cultural experiences. Whether a child has a physical disability, sensory impairment, or other special need also contributes to his uniqueness. The first section of this chapter has already described how relationships contribute to a young child's uniqueness. This section considers both the impact of his genetic predispositions for responding to the world and the impact of the child's experiences on his development.

Temperament is a window on the child.

Temperament refers to a child's individual way of approaching and responding to the world. It has been compared to "a personal pair of mental 'colored glasses'" through which a child views and responds to the world (Herschkowitz and Herschkowitz 2002). Although temperament is inborn, children who are nurtured by understanding and accepting adults are able to go beyond responses typical of their temperament.

Researchers Thomas and Chess (1977) have identified nine temperament traits: how

"Wherever they occur, efforts to enhance the well-being of infants and toddlers must take into account the two dominant characteristics of our youngest children: first, that they can do so little; and second, that they can do so much. Because they can do so little, infants and toddlers need almost constant attention and care. Keeping them nourished, warm, dry, and safe, requires prodigious effort. . . . But because they can do so much, simply keeping them nourished, warm, dry, and safe is not sufficient. The kind of care young children receive, and the settings in which they spend their days, matter a great deal."

—R. Shore, *What Kids Need: Today's Best Ideas for Nurturing, Teaching, and Protecting Young Children*

Sensory and Motor Differences

Just as there are differences in temperament, each child also differs in how he or she takes in and responds to information from the senses about the world and his or her own body. We see this in babies who become distressed by clanging noises or who wiggle uncomfortably when waistbands fit closely or who react negatively to a caregiver's new cologne. The way that sensory information is processed and organized, as well as differences in quality of muscle tone, affects a child's motor responses to people and objects in the environment. These differences are part of the child's neurological make-up and, in most cases, in the normal range. How a child receives and organizes sensory input and how she organizes motor responses can have a profound effect on how she relates to others and how she regulates behavior. Recognizing a child's unique pattern of sensory preferences and tolerances is another step in individualizing care.

— Adapted from G. Williamson and M. Anzalone, *Sensory Integration and Self-Regulation in Infants and Toddlers*

active the child is, how regular she is in her eating and sleep patterns, how adaptable she is, how positive her mood tends to be, whether she approaches new situations readily or is slow to warm up to them, how sensitive she is to stimulation, how intensely she reacts to stimulation, or how persistent or how distractible she tends to be.

Temperament traits cluster together to create distinct styles of approaching and responding to people and situations. For example, one child may readily approach new situations while also expressing her feelings intensely. A second child may be adaptable and may react quietly to things; and a third child may be slow to warm up to new situations and be highly sensitive to stimulation or often fussy. Each of these children will develop unique relationships that will depend, in part, on how well the adults' responses fit the child's temperament style. When the adult adapts to the child's temperament, the

better the fit and the more positive their developing relationship is likely to be.

Different temperaments may match more or less well with group-care settings, too. A child with an active, exuberant temperament may thrive in a setting where he can freely explore the environment and assert himself. However, in a setting without a positive outlet for his exuberant approach to people and things, his behavior may be viewed as challenging by teachers, whereas a child who is adaptable and quiet may be considered "easy." Since programs usually serve groups of children, they have to be flexible enough to accommodate children with vastly different temperaments.

Culture, language, and developmental differences contribute to the child's uniqueness.

A family's culture and language contribute to a child's learning and development in many ways. Culturally based experiences affect not only young children's food preferences, language development, and social relations but also the ways in which children take in and react to new information and ideas. Children may solve problems by working with others or by working alone. When learning language, they learn cultural rules—when to listen and speak, how to show respect, and which words are appropriate and which ones are inappropriate. Children's experiences at home and in the community influence their reactions to infant/toddler settings. A setting may be familiar to a child, or it may be unfamiliar or even frightening. For instance, if a child is from a family that talks loudly and loves music and dancing, she may feel surprised and unsure in a setting where the teacher speaks in quiet tones and dancing is not encouraged. This experience can easily happen the other way around. A child from a generally quiet family may enter a loud and busy infant/toddler setting and quickly feel sensory overload. In either case the teacher's understanding of the child's home culture and language will enable the teacher to make the infant/toddler group-care setting more familiar and comfortable for the child.

Each child will approach and explore his or her environment and relationships differently. Some children need specialized support from an attentive adult to help them actively explore their worlds and build relationships with other people. Other children naturally seek out these experiences through self-discovery and activity. Although most children generally follow a fairly similar developmental path, some children have differences in their development due to their disability, experiences, or inborn traits. Understanding each child's development is part of the joy and responsibility of the teacher. If the child's development varies from the expected path, the teacher needs to monitor it, communicate with the family, and determine how best to support the child. If a child is receiving early intervention services, a team of people, including family members, will be able to provide guidance and insight about the unique characteristics of each child (Carr and Hanson 2001).

Conclusion

The four major insights described in this chapter confirm and expand on what the early childhood profession already knows from years of practice. Through responsive care, teachers focus on establishing secure relationships with infants and toddlers. Secure relationships become the base for young children's exploration and learning across all domains or areas of development. Being responsive to all infants and toddlers requires keeping the whole child in view. A teacher who understands that children are both competent and vulnerable at all times relates to children as active, motivated learners while providing loving care that ensures their safety and well-being. Being responsive also means getting to know each child as the unique person she is. From the family and through observation, teachers learn that each child's abilities, rate of development, and ways of relating to others combine to make her like no other child. One of the greatest challenges and rewards of teaching is finding the approach that best facilitates each child's unique path of learning and development.

Chapter 3
The Role of the Infant Care Teacher

For children in an infant/toddler program, the teacher is the center of their experience. The teacher notices when children are hungry or tired and takes care of them. As children grow and change, the teacher puts materials in the indoor and outdoor environments that introduce new opportunities for exploration and discovery. When a young infant reaches out to touch another baby, the teacher is nearby—smiling, providing encouragement, and helping the children learn how to be with each other.

The teacher is at once a nurturer, a guide, a supporter, an encourager, an observer, a planner, a provider of new experiences, a safe lap, and a listener. The teacher helps the children feel that they are in a place that was made just for them.

Teachers in high-quality settings, both family child care homes and centers, bring many important attributes to the job of guiding infant and toddler learning and development (Pawl 1990b). These attributes include an understanding of child development, the ability to observe and identify each child's unique characteristics, interpersonal skills to support relationships with families and colleagues, and a professional commitment to ongoing learning. High-quality infant/toddler programs help teachers focus on the child; work together with the family, as described in Chapter 1; and understand the child's path of development, as described in Chapter 2.

Every interaction with an infant or toddler may present new possibilities for supporting the child's development. The child is a dynamic and active person who responds to each interaction and experience in a unique way. For the teacher every moment provides an opportunity to learn—to find ways to cultivate the potential in every child. Through embracing their role as learners, teachers become more effective. Through observing, asking questions, listening, and reflecting, they learn from the children and from the children's families and build on their knowledge and skills. Other sources of professional development for teachers include keeping up-to-date on child development information; attending training on infant/toddler care and education; working with specialists in early intervention, social services, and health care; and reflecting on their work.

Essential curriculum areas are as follows:

- Physical development and learning
  – Fine motor
  – Hand–eye coordination
  – Gross motor
- Identity formation
  – Self-awareness
  – Self-expression
- Social–emotional development and learning
  – Responsive caregiving
  – Temperament and individual differences in group care
  – Meeting children's emotional needs

  – Guidance and discipline with infants and toddlers in group care
- Language and communication development and learning
  – Child-directed speech
  – Self-talk and parallel talk
  – Nonverbal communication
  – Expansion of child language
  – Use of books and stories with infants and toddlers
  – Singing (with finger play and gestures), rhyming games, and other ways to make language engaging and playful
  – Imitation games with language (e.g., mirroring and highlighting)
  – Warning signs
- Cognitive development and learning
  – Spatial relationships
  – Cause-and-effect relationships
  – Means/ends relationships
  – Intellectual scheme development
  – Imitation
- Effective group-care strategies
  – Primary care and continuity of care
  – Group size and personalized care
  – Daily routines in group-care settings
  – Health and safety
  – Environments for group care
- Curriculum
  – Curriculum planning
  – Environments
  – Interactions
- Families and communities
  – Working with children with special needs or other disabilities
  – Developing community partnerships
  – Being responsive to diversity

Self-Awareness and Reflection

Self-awareness and reflection help teachers understand their strong feelings to protect children. Teachers also gain insights into their attitudes about different approaches to infant care and the inclusion of children with disabilities or other special needs. Childhood experiences often shape one's beliefs about educating and nurturing children. For example, a teacher who was brought up to sit quietly and listen may believe that all children should be raised that way. Teachers who are unaware of the influence of their childhood experiences may feel comfortable only with practices with which they are familiar. Reflection enables teachers to appreciate the impact of their own backgrounds and upbringing on their practices and become open to the value of other approaches. Awareness of one's beliefs helps teachers to communicate openly with families (Gonzales-Mena 1997).

As part of professional development, effective teachers learn from exploring their feelings about children with disabilities or other special needs. Teachers who are not completely aware of their attitudes may fear that they would not know how to care for a child with a disability and could do something harmful or inappropriate. Self-awareness helps teachers overcome any fearful responses and increases their openness to the benefits of inclusion for all children and families (Carr and Hanson 2001; *Map to Inclusive Child Care Project* 2001; *Barriers to Inclusive Child Care* 2001).

Self-awareness also enhances teachers' skills in day-to-day interactions with children.

For example, some teachers learn that they are overly concerned for the children's safety. This exaggerated concern may lead them to restrict the children's opportunities to test their developing abilities. Teachers who become aware of their emotional reactions discover ways of ensuring safety while allowing children to try out new challenges. Similarly, teachers may be unaware that their feelings about a child who is temperamentally sensitive or distractible may interfere with their relationship with that child. When they become aware of their feelings, teachers open up to the child and appreciate the child's unique strengths, needs, and interests (Lally and others 1995).

Awareness of one's emotional responses is essential for teachers when concerns about the child's well-being arise. At times, stress and negative emotions may interfere with a family's ability to nurture their child and, in response, a teacher's impulse to protect the child may become magnified. To interact respectfully with the family and to find ways to support the family and their child, teachers need to work on learning about the family's perspective and understanding their own emotional responses (Pawl 1990b).

Self-awareness and reflection are prerequisites to careful observation of children, as personal feelings can often cloud what

Taking Time to Listen

Natalie, an infant care teacher, has made a point to listen to and support the parents in her classroom. As sixteen-year-old Xiumei arrives at the center with her four-month-old daughter, Yingying, tears are streaming down Xiumei's face. Teacher Natalie greets her with a tender smile and asks Xiumei how she is doing. Natalie knows, because they have talked a lot in the past several weeks, that Xiumei is under tremendous pressure. She stops and listens to Xiumei's story of her morning. After she put Yingying in the stroller and rushed out the door to make the 6:30 a.m. bus, Xiumei

realized that she had forgotten Yingying's blanket. She could not go back because she had to get Yingying to the center and hurry to class. Mrs. Ruiz, her teacher for vocational training, had already told Xiumei if she was late again she would have to repeat the class.

So many thoughts are running through Xiumei's mind, including Yingying, class, getting a job, and the many bills she has to pay. If Xiumei has to take this class again, she will not get the job at the local hospital. Natalie acknowledges that Xiumei's morning sounds really stressful and hands her a box of tissues.

With permission Natalie gently takes Yingying after Xiumei gives her a kiss on the forehead and wraps her in a blanket that belongs to the center. Natalie asks Xiumei if she wants to take a moment to sit on the couch and catch her breath. Xiumei sadly says she would like to, but she can't. From past experiences Natalie has learned that Xiumei will seek comfort from others outside of her family only when she feels she really needs it. In a supportive voice Natalie says she understands and tells Xiumei to "hang in there," things will work out, and Yingying is in good hands.

teachers see. Acting on personal feelings can also have a negative impact on the quality of care and education teachers provide. For example, a teacher experiencing stress in her personal life and feeling overwhelmed may be annoyed by a child's clinginess and react angrily rather than taking time to think about what might be going on with him and how she can help him feel secure. Teachers who become aware of their personal feelings through reflection are better equipped to focus on the children and the families and provide responsive care and education.

The Infant Care Teacher's Role

Effective teaching is rooted in an understanding that infants and toddlers are active, motivated learners who have their own curriculum. To facilitate discovery and exploration, teachers adapt to the strengths, abilities, needs, and interests of individual children. A responsive approach with every child provides the key to including children with disabilities or other special needs in infant/toddler programs. The major responsibilities of teachers are as follows:

- Build and maintain positive relationships with families.
- Build and maintain positive relationships with children.
- Prepare the environment.
- Establish predictable, consistent routines.
- Appreciate physical activity as learning.

- Nurture social–emotional growth and socialization.
- Foster cognitive development, language development, and communication.
- Implement a curriculum process.

Build and Maintain Positive Relationships with Families

Positive relationships with families foster two-way communication. When teachers establish an honest, caring, and understanding interchange with family members, children's experiences in the infant/toddler setting become more predictable for them. As described in Chapter 1, discussions with family members help teachers to find out about their approach to care and the child's unique characteristics and experiences. This two-way sharing of information allows teachers to interact with infants and toddlers in familiar ways and to build connections between home and the infant/toddler program throughout the child's enrollment.

Build and Maintain Positive Relationships with Children

Teachers build meaningful relationships with children during ordinary, everyday interactions. A mutual gaze with a four-month-

old baby, a moment of eye contact with a twelve-month-old child scooting across the room, the acknowledgment of a two-year-old's interest in his image in the mirror—such actions occur every day in infant/toddler programs. In one instance a child feels more secure, in another a child becomes more willing to explore, and in a third a child gains a stronger sense of self. Teachers who are responsive as they develop relationships with infants and toddlers appear to work magic. But underneath the magic are a compassionate interest in each child, careful observations, a commitment to children and families, and a thoughtful approach to supporting development and learning.

Prepare the Environment

The physical environment communicates powerful messages to infants and toddlers. The design of children's environments is crucial because it affects children in many ways, including their physical and emotional safety and learning experiences. Well-designed environments:

Responsive Relationships at Different Ages and Stages

Four-month-old Augustin relaxes and gazes into the eyes of his teacher, Rita. He is resting comfortably in her arms after having a bottle. Rita gazes back and smiles and says, "Mmm, Augustin, you seem quite content. Let's sit here for a moment together." After a few moments Rita tells Augustin she will place him in his crib for a nap and that she will be nearby to keep an eye on him while he sleeps. He knows her well, and this routine is familiar to him. Rita has other babies to care for too, but when he is in her arms, Augustin feels as if he is the only baby in the world. Rita also helps him to be safe and comfortable when he is on the floor with the other children, who are a bit older. For Augustin, Rita is an anchor.

Twelve-month-old Ana scoots across the room, looking intently at a red toy truck on a low shelf. She looks back at her teacher. Mrs. Lopez smiles and nods. Ana is practicing being on her own, an experience new to her. She will probably return to Mrs. Lopez's lap in a few moments. Mrs. Lopez knows that Ana started scooting just a few days ago at home. Her mom and dad were excited about seeing Ana, who was born with spina bifida, start scooting and moving around on her own. When Mrs. Lopez organized her living room into a child care home, she knew that babies would be exploring every inch of available space. She worked on making it safe, interesting, and flexible enough to grow and adapt with the children in her care. As a result, Ana can explore in her own time, in her own way. When Ana discovers blocks inside the truck, she makes a happy sound. Mrs. Lopez acts surprised ("My goodness, there are three blocks in that truck") even though she put them there with Ana in mind.

As two-year-old Lin gazes into the mirror, she smiles at herself and says, "Lin, that is Lin." Her teacher, Jamal, says, "Yes, a reflection of Lin in the mirror and look, here's Jamal in the mirror too!" Lin scans the room behind her in the mirror and sees that Emma is at the top of the slide. "Emma slide," she says to Jamal. They both turn from the mirror and look as Emma slides her favorite doll down the slide. Jamal notes that Lin is using the mirror as a tool to survey the room. As quick as a cat, Lin darts across the room and catches Emma's doll at the bottom of the slide. Jamal moves with her to see what will happen next. Emma howls, "Mine!" Lin looks from the doll to Emma, to Jamal. She offers the doll to Emma and says, "More?" Emma smiles, and the game of sliding the doll together begins. Jamal breathes a sigh of relief and smiles to himself. He has intervened many times in conflicts between Lin and Emma, and it is a joy to see their friendship develop. He looks forward to telling their families about the game they invented.

- Are safe and appropriately challenging.
- Provide appropriate choices for the children—not too many or too few.
- Invite children to move freely—instead of limiting their ability to move.
- Are furnished with chairs and other equipment the right size—not too big or too small.
- Are adapted to all children in the group so that every child can participate in the daily experiences.
- Offer peaceful places, areas to be active, and places to explore materials—rather than one large, cluttered room.
- Display pictures of the children, their families, and their community—rather than things that are unfamiliar to the children and lack personal meaning.

- Are stable and predictable—because constant changes can be confusing to infants and toddlers.

Creating an environment that matches the children's developing abilities and interests requires careful observation and thoughtful planning (Torelli and Durrett 1998). The goal for teachers is to make everything in the environment say to the children, "This place is for you."

Set up the environment for learning and development. In designing the environment, teachers set the stage for learning and development (*Infant/Toddler Caregiving: A Guide to Setting Up Environments* 1990). The environment affects every area of growth, including motor development, social–emotional development, language development, and cognitive learning and development. Teachers in high-quality programs work together with families to create a predictable, familiar, and meaningful environment for the children. Effective teachers place materials indoors and outdoors that offer a rich variety of possibilities for movement, exploration, and discovery. They observe which kinds of materials hold children's attention and introduce slightly different yet related things. They notice the skills a child is trying to master and find ways for that child to practice them. Teachers also need to ensure that children who want private time by themselves have places to move away from the group yet can still be supervised. In a toddler program, for example, lace curtains were hung under a loft to allow teachers to see a child who wants to be in a private place.

One of the most important principles of preparing the environment is to make adaptations for every child in the group. This principle supports responsive care and education. It also facilitates the inclusion of infants and toddlers with disabilities or other special needs. An environment that is adapted to the developing abilities and strengths of individual children makes possible the full participation of every child (Torelli 2002).

Create a healthy and safe environment. Infant care teachers support learning and development by maintaining a safe and healthy environment for infants and toddlers. Key health practices include frequent cleaning and sanitizing of surfaces, play materials, and equipment. Teachers need to inspect the environment regularly for safety hazards, such as mushrooms growing in the play yard or slippery wet floors in the bathroom. Inspections and other measures prevent accidents and injuries.

Establish Predictable, Consistent Caregiving Routines

The heart of the infant/toddler curriculum lies in the daily caregiving routines (Lally and others 1995). Daily routines, such as diapering, dressing, feeding, napping, and even wiping a nose, offer rich opportunities for engaging the child's attention and cooperation (an important early step in socialization and guidance), for learning, and for deepening relationships.

Personalize caregiving routines. The intimate, one-to-one time during caregiving allows teachers to personalize interactions with each child. Because each child has different experiences at home with routines, communication with the child's family members helps to ensure continuity between home and the infant/toddler setting. For example, one infant may appreciate talking and laughing during care activities, and another child may be more quiet, slow-moving, and attentive to the teacher's actions.

Appreciate the ordinary as extraordinary. Children under three do not distinguish routine chores from play or work or adventure the way adults do. For children every event is as sensually rich and important as the next. But ordinary routines quickly become special to children because they are ordinary; they are repeated over and over. Children recognize them. They come to rely on them to give rhythm and order to their lives. They become familiar with the sequence of activities that make up each different chore. They begin to join in whatever way they can. Through their participation in everyday activities, children begin to develop ideas about past and future, beginning, middle, and end, space and time, cause and effect, pattern and meaning, self and other, friend and strangers that will help them one day sort out their experiences the way adults do (Dombro and Wallach 2001).

Routines become familiar events in the day that provide predictability and security. Even young infants come to anticipate the sequence of events. A nap, for example,

Adapt to the Unexpected

Because of the unpredictability of young children's interests, teachers frequently have to create a balance between being predictable and being flexible in carrying out the daily activities. In a program for older toddlers, for example, when the children were playing outside, a grandfather stopped by unexpectedly and dropped off a fresh bale of hay. The toddlers were fascinated with the hay. They pulled the bale to shreds and then began to stuff the hay into openings under the slide. Observing their cooperative play, focus, and passion, their teacher decided to let the outside time last longer that morning. This change meant that lunch and nap times were a little late. When family members came to pick children up at the end of the day, their children took them to the playground to look into the openings and see the hay.

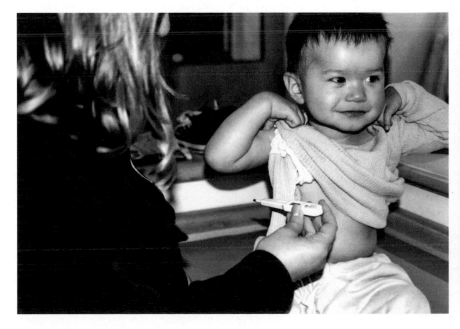

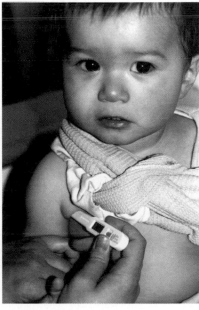

follows a bottle and some time in the teacher's lap. Routines should be predictable but also flexible enough to allow for changes.

Attend to health and safety during routines. During routines teachers must carefully maintain healthful and safe practices to protect both children and adults and to minimize absences due to illness or injuries. Frequent hand-washing is a highly effective measure to reduce the incidence of communicable diseases. Teachers should work with families and specialists and follow through on any procedures or precautions that may be required when a child has a special health need.

Appreciate Physical Activity as Learning

Because infants and toddlers are continually learning with their bodies, teachers need to attend to motor development and learning in their daily interactions. Infants and toddlers make many important discoveries about people, objects, gravity, spatial relationships, and their capabilities and limits through freely moving their bodies (Gopnik, Meltzoff, and Kuhl 2000). Children who have a physical disability move in whatever ways they can. Family members and specialists help teachers learn how to assist a child who has a physical disability with movement and exploration.

Honor the natural process of physical development. Physical development unfolds naturally and usually does not need to be taught. Infants and toddlers are motivated to

move their bodies to make discoveries. Teachers can support this process by remaining available to give assistance when children need it. To learn to move and walk, children do not need equipment that in any way restricts their movement. In cases where a child has a disability or other special need and requires special support, a specialist working with the child and family may recommend adaptive equipment.

Teachers support children in making wise choices by preparing a safe yet appropriately challenging environment and staying available. Because children are more likely to fall and get hurt when they have been put in places they did not get to themselves, teachers should avoid placing children on equipment or into positions that they cannot yet manage on their own. A safe environment frees teachers to enjoy and support an infant's developing abilities by watching, smiling, and talking about what the child is doing.

Plan and prepare to support children's free, active movement. When teachers understand that young children must move, they facilitate movement by observing each child's development and by looking ahead to what each child might do next. When planned for, children's interest in actively moving their bodies can be enjoyed and appreciated and not considered a disruption. Infants and toddlers test their abilities frequently and change quickly. To keep the child safe and allow free choices and appropriate risk taking, teachers

need to stay available and modify the environment when necessary. In programs with mixed-age groups and with children of diverse abilities, teachers need to consider all the children in the group and make arrangements for their emerging abilities.

For an infant who is crawling, a low platform or ramp that raises the child only a few inches from the floor is an appropriate challenge. Later, as the infant begins to pull up on objects and move along them, a teacher might provide a low table that is the right height for "cruising." Toddlers have jokingly been called "furniture movers," as many of them love to push heavy objects, such as chairs and tables, around. When teachers respond to children's natural urge to move, they can do it in a way that works for both the children and the teachers. A teacher who, for safety reasons, does not want toddlers pushing furniture might offer crates or boxes to push. Learning and discovery happen when children are physically active; teachers who understand and appreciate this fact find many ways to support physical activity (*Infant/Toddler Caregiving: A Guide to Setting up Environments* 1990).

Nurture Social–Emotional Growth and Socialization

Early social–emotional development has a major impact on all domains of learning and development (Greenspan 1997). Teachers nurture a child's social and emotional health in a variety of ways, including supporting identity development, providing emotional support, facilitating socialization, and giving guidance.

Support identity development. Teachers support identity development by letting the child know that his family and his home language are important. Ways of communicating an appreciation and understanding of the child's developing identity include placing photos of his family in the classroom, engaging in simple rituals at mealtime or naptime that are similar to rituals at home, and speaking the child's home language or saying a few familiar words in the child's home language.

The manner in which teachers handle routines has a powerful effect on the child's developing identity. Consistent, prompt, and nurturing responses to the young infant's cries communicate to the child that her actions make

a difference. The child begins to see herself as someone who can make things happen. Teachers who invite the child to be an active participant in routines let him know that he has an important role to play in his care. Through participation in routines, the child learns that he is someone who can cooperate with others. This approach to routines strengthens the child's self-confidence and makes the experience enjoyable for both the child and the teacher.

An essential part of supporting identity development is recognizing and appreciating what a child is doing and can do (Ramey and Ramey 1999). If teachers are chiefly concerned with what a child cannot yet do, they may focus their educational efforts on skills far beyond the child's developing abilities to the detriment of her sense of self. When teachers base their educational approach on a child's strengths and interests, they validate the child as an active learner and help her to see herself as a capable person.

Provide emotional support. When caring for infants and toddlers in groups, the teacher plays a key role in the emotional climate of the room. When a child observes her family members talking and smiling with her teacher, she is likely to feel safe and comfortable with that teacher. By talking about the child's mommy or grandmother, the teacher encourages the child to think of them and remember her connection to her family. The child looks

to the teacher when she is excited to share a discovery or when she needs help. A warm, positive response from the teacher lets the child know her discoveries are important and that her needs will be met. When the teacher speaks in a nurturing tone to other children, the child sees that the teacher relates to everyone in the group with respect and genuine interest.

Facilitate socialization and give guidance. An important part of the teacher's role is to facilitate socialization in the infant/toddler setting. Socialization means to help children learn to participate in the life of the group.

Infants and toddlers in groups form relationships and become friends. These relationships may present them with their first experiences of feeling affection for a friend, feeling frustration with someone who gets in the way or takes away a toy, and receiving and giving empathy and help. Infants and toddlers in groups are learning to be together and to do things together.

Teachers can help infants and toddlers learn to adapt to the group and become socially competent. For example, a teacher can guide an infant who is reaching for the face of another infant to touch gently. Or the teacher can communicate an understanding of an older child's negative feelings toward a friend, helping the child gain a sense of calm. The environment should be set up so that children have enough materials (to minimize disputes of possession) but are not overwhelmed by too many things or too much stimulation. Quiet places that accommodate two or three children enable them to focus on one another and enjoy their play together.

Interacting with other adults gives teachers another powerful way to facilitate socialization. As children observe teachers interacting with family members, program leaders, other staff, and volunteers, the children are learning how people treat each other.

Foster Cognitive Development, Language Development, and Communication

Infants develop intellectually and learn to communicate through relationships and exploration of the environment. Their teachers support intellectual and language development in their daily interactions with children by recognizing discovery and learning, helping children explore ideas and symbols, and nurturing a love of books and stories.

Recognize discovery and learning. As they explore and try to manipulate things, infants and toddlers constantly make discoveries (*How People Learn* 1999). For infants and toddlers, everything is new. They are learning about cause and effect, the use of tools, the permanent nature of objects even when out of sight, and how things fit in space. They also constantly learn new strategies for exploring and acting on things through imitation and experimentation. They learn by touching, mouthing, banging, and squeezing things. By observing infants and toddlers, teachers can see the discovery process at work. Teachers who recognize the discovery process are more likely to introduce experiences and materials that allow children to explore their interests further. Effective teachers respect the exploration and experimentation of infants and toddlers as they would respect the work of a scientist. They avoid interrupting the children and give them time to pursue their interests. When a child senses that her teacher appreciates her interest in the world, she continues to develop as a self-confident learner and keeps building her competence.

Help children explore ideas and symbols. As infants and toddlers investigate physical environments and relationships, they also explore ideas and symbols (*How People Learn* 1999; Bruner 1983). Conversations with adults about objects and activities in their daily lives help children come to know the names for things (*cat, kitten, ball*) and for categories of things (animals, baby animals, toys). They begin to grasp the rules that govern language (one cat, many cats). In their everyday interactions with adults, they find countless opportunities to explore the nature of nonverbal and verbal communication.

The teacher notes when a child is interested in communicating and responds, such as when an infant crawls into the teacher's lap and tugs on her chin, and the teacher nods and laughs and says, "You pulled my chin!" The teacher can expand on a child's communication. When a child is saying, "Ba ba" and

pointing to the ball, the teacher may add, "Yes, ball. You see the red ball." Singing, rhyming, finger plays, and word games fascinate infants and toddlers and help them to enjoy language and to feel comfortable in trying new ways to communicate.

Experience with language is critically important for infants and toddlers. By being responsive to the children's efforts to communicate and using language regularly with them, adults foster language development. Experience with language also builds young children's vocabularies, which contributes to learning to read when they are much older. Just as important, communication between teacher and child makes their relationship more meaningful.

Children whose family's primary language is different from the language spoken in the infant/toddler setting benefit when they continue to learn their home language (*Improving Schooling for Language-Minority Children* 1997). Research evidence suggests that development of a first language serves as a foundation for acquisition of a second language. Experiences with the home language in the infant/toddler setting help to maintain the sounds and meanings of that language for the child. They also convey the teacher's respect for that language as a valid means of communication, support the child's developing identity, and foster communication at home. Research also indicates that bilingual children who learn English as they develop competence in their home language acquire word identification skills that can support learning to read English in elementary school (Ordóñez and others 2002).

During the infant/toddler years, because of diverse learning styles, personalities, levels of motivation, and family experiences, children who are learning both English and their home language will use different strategies and progress at varying rates. Effective infant care teachers need to be patient and consistent when communicating with children who are learning more than one language.

Nurture a love of books and stories: Preliteracy. In addition to communicating with language, teachers can support what is called preliteracy by reading and telling stories when children are interested. Allowing infants and toddlers to explore books in whatever ways they choose—stacking and carrying books around, turning pages, pausing to study a particular page, holding a book upside down,

opening and closing a book, even sucking on a book—helps them to become comfortable with books. Experiences with books increase children's interest in the stories, ideas, and pictures they contain. Children develop an appreciation for the stories and, as they grow older, begin to understand that the symbols on the page convey meaning. The first steps in learning to read happen many years before the child reads his first word. Some of these steps include the moment a child picks out a favorite book and then sits on a teacher's lap, listens with rapt attention, asks a question, points to a picture, or comments about the story (*Starting Out Right* 1999).

Storytelling, which is common in many families and communities, fosters language learning and encourages discovery, pretend play, and the development of an understanding of cultural beliefs and values (Bruner 1996). Children also begin to learn about the structure of stories, which is an important step in the long journey of learning to read.

Implement a Curriculum Process

Teachers who facilitate learning effectively are in tune with infants and toddlers as active, motivated learners. Because they appreciate the child's natural desire to learn, they observe the child's exploration and provide encouragement by their quiet presence. They look for opportunities to expand on each child's interests through their responses to the child. Each moment a teacher responds is part of an ongoing curriculum process.

Observe each child. To facilitate learning and development effectively, infant care teachers need to observe what children do on their own, without setting up a special activity or directing their behavior. Teachers do not have to change the environment or the ways they interact with a child; they just observe the child's ongoing behavior in the care and education setting.

Document observations. Infant care teachers record their observations by (1) taking notes or photos or by videotaping the children during activities; (2) setting time aside for later documentation; or (3) collecting things older toddlers create. Teachers often work together to document their observations in ways that do not interfere with the teachers' time with the children or disrupt the flow of the day.

Assess children's developmental progress. An integral part of the curriculum process is assessing each child's development. The California Department of Education's Desired Results Developmental Profile-Revised (DRDP-R) is an assessment tool that makes use of observation records. Teachers who already record observations do not have to do additional activities with the children to complete the profile. The information gained from completing the DRDP-R for each child can be used by teachers to guide their observations and plan how to continue support of their learning and development. In addition, periodic assessments using the DRDP-R allow teachers to track how the curriculum process is helping children learn and develop over time.

Reflect on observations. Infant care teachers study their observation records, documentation, and assessment information both individually and with colleagues and family members. Taking time to slow down, review, and think about each child's behavior, temperament, learning interests, developmental profile, and needs helps teachers deepen their understanding and appreciation of each child and gives them ideas on how to continue to support that child's learning and development.

Develop ideas and make plans. This important part of the process can be exciting and invigorating for teachers as they come up with ideas and think about how they might adapt the environment or routines or introduce a new routine or material based on observations, notes, DRDP-R information, reflection, and discussion. Part of the planning process includes reducing the list of ideas to one or two that relate directly to the interests and abilities of a child or a small group of children. Once teachers have a plan for the next step in supporting a child's learning and

The Curriculum Process in Action

Through observation, documentation, assessment, reflection, and planning, a team of teachers decided that a small group of toddlers were ready to try to grasp things above their heads and swing their bodies forward and backward. They had noted, in particular, that the children had been trying to swing from a bar below the changing table. Believing that allowing them to play in the changing area would be unsanitary and inappropriate, the teachers decided to find another place where the toddlers could pursue their interest in swinging their bodies.

They identified a railing on the porch at about the same height as the bar below the changing table. They moved some equipment away from the porch railing and placed a rubber mat below it. Once these changes were made, the teachers observed that the children frequently reached up to the rail and lifted their feet to swing from the porch railing. The children enjoyed doing this activity alone and together.

Now, when children enter the diapering area to try to swing from the rail there, they can be redirected to the porch railing. The children have a place that is safe, sanitary, and appropriately challenging to try out their developing motor abilities. The teachers continue to observe, document, and reflect on the children's use of the railing, along with other large motor play, with an eye toward discovering the next challenge to offer the children.

development, they then introduce the adaptation or change in a way that allows the child to make choices and interact freely and creatively with the new material, environmental set-up, or experience.

Implement plans. As teachers try out their plans with the children, the process begins again with observation. Through observation, then documentation, assessment, and reflection, the teachers learn how the children respond to the change in the environment or routine. This dynamic process of ongoing study of the children's learning and development leads to new curriculum ideas to plan and implement.

Through the curriculum process teachers deepen their understanding of the children. They become more sensitive to the need for adapting the environment and being more responsive to the children's evolving interests and abilities.

Conclusion

Teaching infants and toddlers requires learning about child development, the role of the family and community in the child's development, and the impact of a teacher's beliefs, values, and experiences on relationships with children and families. The many responsibilities of teachers include building relationships, providing emotional support, preparing environments for active learners, and facilitating exploration and discovery. As they develop professionally, teachers become skillful observers and increasingly open to learning from others. Although complex and demanding, the role is highly rewarding. In high-quality programs, teachers have the opportunity to experience firsthand the amazing growth of children with whom they have formed close, caring relationships.

Program Leadership and Administration

Program leaders in infant/toddler care and education settings are the hub around which the program revolves. Their policies and actions set the tone for families, children, teachers, and other staff members. In family-oriented programs, leaders create a welcoming place for families and draw family members into the process of reflecting on and planning the program for the children. Through ongoing communication between teachers and supervisors, program leaders work with staff members to solve problems and to improve the quality of care and education they provide. Program leaders ensure that the setting is designed and equipped to facilitate the learning and development of infants and toddlers and that the program's core policies support the growth of positive, respectful relationships.

Operators of family child care homes, whether they have employees or not, are program leaders. In addition to managing their own business, family child care providers create the foundation for their program and carry out the many responsibilities of program leadership.

The major responsibilities of program leaders include setting policies to:

- Establish an emotionally supportive climate for families, children, teachers, and other staff members.

- Foster the professional growth of the teachers and the continuous improvement of the program.

- Establish and maintain relations with the larger community and attend to business and funding concerns.

- Manage the facilities, attend to health and safety, comply with regulations and laws, and administer a system for assessment and monitoring.

To be effective in carrying out these responsibilities, leaders must have a vision of high-quality care and education that includes everyone—children, families, teachers, and other staff members. This chapter describes an overall approach to program leadership and administration and identifies policies and practices of effective program leaders.

Leadership

Effective leaders seek to create a program that is open to everyone's participation and respects different perspectives on participation. Through reflecting on the program together, sharing ideas, and listening to one another's perspectives, families and staff can discover how to work together to promote the learning and development of the children. A leader who respects and listens to the opinions and ideas of everyone and who also facilitates communication and discussion creates opportunities for families and staff to learn from each other. One of the greatest challenges for a leader is to help families and staff members find ways to move forward together with a common purpose while respecting diversity. To meet this challenge the leader works to solicit ideas from families and staff members and to develop policies and procedures that are responsive to their feedback.

While being respectful and responsive to families and staff, a program leader cannot accommodate every wish or concern of a family member or a teacher. The leader must balance the wishes of families and staff

---

Different Ways of Participating

Sonja had tried something new today in the staff meeting—having teachers role-play a conference with family members. She wanted to help the teachers find ways to talk about potentially difficult topics with family members. The activity did not go the way she planned. She asked Jasmine to play the parent of a toddler who bit another child. This behavior happened in Jasmine's classroom, and Sonja thought it might help Jasmine to wear the mother's shoes for this exercise. Jasmine had never done a role play before. She had never even heard of it.

At first, Sonja strongly encouraged Jasmine to participate. Sonja felt that Jasmine was just being stubborn or shy. Jasmine got up and sat in front of everybody, but before she spoke, she started to cry silently. Sonja felt terrible. She did not know what to do for a moment. Liz, Jasmine's co-teacher, handed Jasmine a tissue and led her out of the room. Sonja looked at the group and said, "I am sorry. I thought it was a good idea." Everyone was quiet.

When Jasmine and Liz returned a few minutes later, Liz spoke for Jasmine. Jasmine had asked Liz to explain that she came from a religious and cultural community in which being the center of attention and acting like some- one else was just unheard of. It was shameful behavior. Hugo, a new teacher in the infant room, suggested that, instead of doing role plays, they talk about how parents and other family members might feel in a conference with the teacher and how the teacher might help them to feel more comfortable. Sonja smiled at Hugo and felt relieved as the other staff members agreed to the idea. Sonja suggested that if anyone had an idea but did not want to speak out, he or she could give the idea in writing to her.

members with the legal requirements and financial considerations of the program and widely accepted standards for high-quality care and education. Sometimes a program leader must make an unpopular decision or set an unpopular policy—to avoid doing so would be irresponsible. The key for the leader is to communicate in a straightforward, clear manner and, insofar as possible, to adapt to concerns of the families and staff members when setting policies and making decisions.

Policies Supportive of Teachers' Professional Growth

The professional development of teachers is essential for high-quality care and education. The National Institute of Child Health and Human Development Early Childhood Research Network (1999) found that, by three years of age, children whose teachers have more job-related training or formal education score higher in areas of language comprehension and school readiness and have fewer behavior problems. With teachers who are better prepared, infants develop stronger expressive language skills (Burchinal and others 1996), and both infants and toddlers are more likely to engage in language activities, complex play with objects, and creative activities in child care settings (Howes 1997).

Effective program leaders recognize the crucial role of the professional development of teachers. Such leaders create learning opportunities for teachers and support their efforts to continue their education. Such leaders also take full advantage of on-site consultation,

technical assistance, and training that is available to their program. If feasible, programs should provide incentives for teachers to continue their education. Part of the leader's job is to stay current on incentives and learning opportunities for teachers in the larger community. That information should be regularly given to staff members, and an effort should be made to allow them to participate in professional development outside the program.

Just as important as the professional development of teachers is the continued growth of the program leader. Participation in professional development enables the program leader both to understand what teachers are learning and to support the implementation of the latest information on high-quality care and education. Teachers appreciate when their program leader stays current on infant development and care, and they look to that person as a model for their own professional growth.

Because families are reassured when they sense that the program is of high quality, program leaders are responsible for communicating with families about the continuing professional development of the staff. Information about the policies that support the staff's professional growth can be conveyed to families in meetings, conversations, the program's handbook, and other written materials. The views of families should be considered in determining the focus of on-site

technical assistance and training. Often, ideas from family members or concerns they express help leaders identify priorities for strengthening the program.

The program leader has to make sure that professional development remains a priority in the face of daily demands that are sure to arise. A hallmark of leadership is to provide and protect regular times for conversation and reflection with teachers, individually and as a group. The time and attention given to professional growth and the leader's approach to it will shape staff interactions with the children and families and will enhance the program's quality of care and education.

Reflective Supervision

Reflective supervision means that the teachers' supervisor—often the program leader—and teachers have regular conversations in which they explore together the many complex feelings, thoughts, and issues that arise in working with young children and families and with other staff members. In these

conversations, the supervisor helps teachers find answers to their questions. The supervisor adapts the manner in which she works with staff based on a variety of factors. The supervisor's approach will depend on the personal and professional experiences of staff members; their style of interacting with others; and the particular situation in which they are providing services to infants, toddlers, and their families.

The supervisor also offers support as teachers decide how to apply new insights and information to their work with children and families. When supervisors listen carefully, pause to think about what teachers say, ask questions, and share ideas, teachers experience the kind of trusting, respectful, and caring

relationship they are being asked to build with children and families.

The reflective process is not just for teachers but for program leaders, too. Supervisors or colleagues within or outside the program can support each other. Family child care providers who work alone can find opportunities for reflective conversations in provider networks or associations or with classmates from child development courses. Interaction between colleagues who serve as peer mentors for each other supports a cycle of positive change.

Reflective supervision creates opportunities for teachers to contribute to the continuing development of the program. The reciprocal nature of reflective supervision enables teachers to clarify issues and problems for program leaders and to identify ways for the program to operate more effectively. Through this process, specific program policies or customs may be reconsidered based on teachers' experiences and suggestions.

Program Policies for High-Quality Care and Education

Among the many ways that program leaders work to achieve high quality is by establishing policies that (1) promote a family-oriented approach; (2) support reflective supervision with staff members; and (3) enable teachers to be responsive to infants and toddlers and their families. The recommended program policies that follow have been developed to foster positive relationships throughout an infant/toddler program. Family child care programs often have two of these policies—primary care and continuity of care—built into their program structures, and many child care centers have found creative ways to administer such policies. For financial and administrative reasons, the policy of ensuring small groups by reducing teacher-to-child ratios and overall group size presents a challenge to programs—and yet the benefits to children, families, and teachers are significant (*Developmentally Appropriate Practice* 1997).

Responsive Care and Education

Being responsive to families is at the heart of the program leader's job. A responsive approach to care and education allows programs to adapt to each unique family, including families with children with disabilities or other special needs. Teachers can become more responsive through staff development opportunities that help them explore their own values. Through learning about their own perspectives, they become more appreciative and accepting of other perspectives, recognizing similarities and differences between their points of view and those of others. Staff development should also focus on working together with the family and specialists who support a child with a disability or other special needs.

Primary Care System

In a primary care system, an infant care teacher is responsible for a small group of children (Bernhardt 2000). This teacher carries out daily care routines, communicates daily with family members, and observes and maintains individual records on each child in the small group. Primary care is usually a team effort in which two teachers work together, each one having primary responsibility for half of the children in the group. (Each teacher is also secondarily responsible for the other teacher's children.) Though primary care is not exclusive, it does give infants and toddlers and their families a chance to come to know one teacher well. The teacher and the infant are able to develop routines together. A teacher would know, for instance, that one child in the primary group likes to place the toy she is holding on a nearby shelf before a diaper change and retrieve it after her diaper is changed and hands are washed. The teacher and the child's family more easily come to know each other, too. When the teacher and the family share their understanding of the child, they find ways to develop continuity between care in the infant/toddler setting and care at home. This type of personalized understanding goes a long way toward helping the infant and family develop a sense of well-being and belonging. The security that develops through primary care frees the child to explore and discover the environment and to develop friendships with other children (Pope and Raikes 2002).

Small-Group Size

A policy for maintaining small groups strengthens the primary-care relationship and fosters the safety, health, and comfort of infants and toddlers (*Caring for Our Children* 2002; *Developmentally Appropriate Practice* 1997; Lally and others 1995). Ideally, a small group of children and two teachers are in a separate room by themselves rather than in a large space with other groups. A good rule of thumb is that the younger the children, the smaller the group should be. When children with disabilities or other special needs are part of the group, the group size should allow teachers to provide the specialized services or care those children may require to participate fully with other children (Carr and Hanson 2001).

Culturally Sensitive Care and Education

Program leaders play a crucial role in enrolling families in the program. Leaders have primary responsibility for developing a system of communication, starting with initial interviews, that is responsive to families who have different values, child-rearing perspectives, and goals for children. Arrangements should be made to communicate in the family's home language if family members speak a language different from the program staff. Ongoing professional staff development and reflective supervision should focus on and support understanding of diverse perspectives and resulting practices. Staff members and family members need time to discuss their different values and goals. When programs accept cultural diversity and sensitively adapt to families of various cultures, they create a climate of trust and understanding. Care for infants and toddlers that connects with their families' beliefs and practices helps individual children feel a sense of belonging in the program.

Inclusion of All Children and Families

Program leaders make a strong statement about being responsive to diverse families when policy and corresponding practice accept all children, including those with disabilities or other special needs. Inclusion means making a commitment to respect all families as unique people whose strengths and needs are in some ways similar and in other ways different from the strengths and needs of other families (*Map to Inclusive Child Care* 2001). Because family members understand their child better than anyone else, family-oriented programs provide a sound approach for including children with disabilities or other special needs. Family members can offer insights into how to adapt the infant/toddler setting to accommodate their child and how to link with early intervention specialists who support his learning and development. Throughout the child's time in the program, the family will be at the center of a collaborative team that includes early intervention specialists and program staff.

Continuity of Care

The term *continuity* is used in many ways in the early childhood field. It refers to caring for children in a way that is similar to the style of care they receive at home. It also refers to helping children make a transition from home to a care and education setting or from one care and education setting to another. In this document *continuity of care* is used to define the length of time that a primary infant care teacher and a small group of children are together: optimally, for the first three years of life, if not longer.

Program leaders can help children and families feel secure by making decisions that aim to maximize continuity. Their policies should provide staff members with the working conditions, supports, and opportunities for professional development and advancement that keep good teachers in their programs and in the field. The goal is for teachers to stay

with the same group of children from the time of enrollment until the children are three years old. This policy allows teachers to deepen

New Ideas Take Time

Marta sighs; she feels tired. It is late at night after the staff meeting at the Tender Hearts Children's Center. Marta wanted to get the staff members excited about changing their child care program to allow groups of children and caregivers to stay together over time. This approach was called *continuity of care.* She learned about the idea at a conference she attended with Lianne, the infant room lead teacher. Lianne and Marta had a long talk on the drive home about how wonderful it would be for children to have time to know each other and their teachers. Continuity of care was supposed to help reduce conflict, which would be really nice. It was also supposed to help children to concentrate more on exploration and learning because they would feel more confident and comfortable when they knew everybody well.

When Marta introduced the idea of children and teachers staying together, the other teachers didn't like the idea at all. One teacher said she only liked working with toddlers, not with little babies. Another teacher asked how a group could stick together when she had a new assistant every few months. A third teacher wondered how it would work when she left on maternity leave the next month. Marta herself began to question the idea when she thought about how much children's enrollment fluctuated, and she wondered how it would work when the teacher-to-child ratios changed as the children grew older.

Lianne pokes her head in Marta's office before heading home and asks, "You all right?" Marta shakes her head and says, "It sounded so good until the staff brought up all those problems and barriers." Lianne nods and says, "Yeah, that meeting was overwhelming, but we can't overcome barriers if we don't know what they are. What if we have another meeting and see if the same people who identified the problems can help us think of some

solutions?" Marta nodded and commented, "You know, if you think of your own children switching teachers all the time and meeting new kids every few months, you want to protect them from that. You want them to feel safe and comfortable. Maybe we could start by asking staff to think about children they know and love. When we were asked to do this at the conference, I started to see things from the child's point of view. If teachers think about staying together with the same group from the child's perspective, instead of from a classroom management perspective, the idea may feel different." Lianne adds, "Maybe we could also ask people for their ideas about how to make things more . . . what was that word the presenter used? 'Continuous' for the children."

They smile at each other, and Marta thanks Lianne for being supportive. They turn out the lights and head out to their cars to go home to their families.

their relationships not only with individual children but also with families. In California continuity of care is especially important as one-third of infants and toddlers in nonparental care spend time in more than one child care arrangement and must already negotiate relationships with several caregivers (Ehrle, Adams, and Tout 2001).

Children also develop close and meaningful relationships with each other over time. When children are cared for primarily by one teacher in a small group over a period of years, they have an opportunity to develop deep and continuing relationships. These relationships provide them with valuable early experiences: caring for others, the feeling of being cared for, negotiating, and cooperating—in other words, learning to live with their peers. Family child care programs that serve mixed-age groups provide infants and toddlers with the rich experience of developing relationships with children of various ages as well as the opportunity to be in the same setting with their brothers and sisters.

Relations with the Surrounding Community

Early care and education programs are important parts of communities. The programs play an essential role that is more than providing child care. As programs develop relationships with individuals and other organizations in the community, all of them have the opportunity to participate in a shared vision. How a community views, nurtures, and educates its children is a key component to community success. Early care and education programs can be a driving force in increasing community awareness and appreciation of children.

Program leaders make their program visible to the community in a variety of ways. One way to make the community aware of the program is to invite volunteers to visit and participate. Another strategy is to partner with community organizations. In addition, making contact with local businesses and letting them know about the program may lead to offers of assistance.

An essential part of the program leader's job is to build relationships with local service providers (Regional Educational Laboratories Early Childhood Collaboration Network 1995). Early intervention specialists may work with the program as they provide support or therapy for children in the program. Health and social service professionals may offer assistance to the program and families. Local public safety services, such as fire and police departments, should be made aware of the program's needs in an emergency situation and consulted when the program develops an emergency preparedness plan.

Administration

Program administration focuses on a wide variety of issues and considerations, including health and safety, the handling of routines, the environment, laws, regulations, accountability, and the assessment of individual children. A thoughtful approach to administrative policies and procedures provides the necessary infrastructure for a program that is responsive to children, families, teachers, and other staff members.

Health and Safety

Keeping infants and toddlers safe and healthy in the context of caring relationships and daily routines includes protecting both

their physical and emotional health. Program leaders set policies and corresponding procedures for health and safety in response to child care licensing standards, current best practices for healthy and safe child care, and suggestions and comments from families and teachers. A program's overall approach to health and safety should take into account the children's developmental abilities and needs because helping children learn about their own limits and abilities and their role in being safe and healthy is important.

Program leaders must establish policies and procedures that protect the health and safety of infants, toddlers, and adults during routine care, such as feeding, mealtimes, diapering, toileting, and napping. Attention must be paid to proper hand-washing; a plan for administering medication when necessary; and proper preparation, handling, and storage of breast milk, formula, and food. Healthful and safe practices during routines assure families that their children are protected and reduce both children's and teachers' absences due to illness.

Teachers and other staff members need frequent updates on health and safety information, such as hand-washing, universal precautions such as using gloves during diaper changes, cardiopulmonary resuscitation (CPR) techniques, and first aid procedures. They also rely on program leaders for proper equipment, supplies, and time for such procedures as cleaning and sanitizing toys and surfaces and responding to any safety or health concern that may arise.

A Well-Designed Environment

Well-designed and appropriately equipped facilities foster the well-being of children and teachers. Everyone thrives in settings that are comfortable, with both child-sized and adult-sized furnishings, natural light, fresh air, and sound-absorption materials that keep noise low. Infants and toddlers should have access to the outdoors, and as much as possible they should be able to move freely between indoors and outdoors. The setting should also be a welcoming place for families and have an area furnished with a couch or comfortable chairs.

Program leaders must make sure that the environment allows visual supervision of all children at all times, including children in nap rooms and the toileting area, and is conveniently arranged for routine care. For example, in centers, plumbing should be located so that teachers can wash hands and help children with toileting in the classroom setting. For proper hygiene, the food preparation area with its own sink must be separate from other areas (in particular, the diapering and toileting areas).

Another aspect of a well-designed environment is a homelike atmosphere. Centers have to work to create this feeling. Family child care homes already provide this atmosphere and do not have to look like miniature child care centers. The family child care provider can creatively adapt the furnishings of her living room, play room, backyard, and kitchen to meet the particular needs and abilities of infants and toddlers without sacrificing the sense of home that is the hallmark of her program.

Laws, Regulations, and Accountability

All infant/toddler programs (with the exception of license-exempt programs) must adhere to laws and regulations. Program leaders are accountable for ensuring that their program meets or exceeds all licensing requirements as well as the requirements of the Americans with Disabilities Act in order to support full participation of children with disabilities or other special needs. Program leaders also have to take steps to ensure that the teachers and other staff members are alert to cases of abuse and neglect and are prepared to act on their suspicions when necessary. Resources are available to help program leaders and teachers understand and meet legal requirements.

Assessment of Children's Development and Program Improvement

As part of engaging in continuous quality improvement, programs assess the developmental progress and learning of infants and toddlers. Programs funded by the California Department of Education use the Desired Results Developmental Profile-Revised assessment instrument. The insights gained through assessments aid teachers in their efforts to plan appropriate learning environments and offer engaging materials to children. The assessment of children's development also helps teachers and family members identify children who need to be referred for further assessment. Periodic assessment of children's development provides a firm basis on which to make a referral.

Effective assessment of children should include information from family members, teachers, and program leaders. Teachers or program leaders usually have primary responsibility for ongoing collection of information on children's learning and development. Family members may participate in the documentation of their children's learning and development. They review the assessment records with teachers and program leaders and participate in planning learning experiences based on the assessment information.

Conclusion

Effective program leadership and administration create the foundation for the growth of positive relationships. A program's climate is most influenced by the approach taken by the program leader. The job requires being attentive and responsive to families, children, teachers, and other staff members. It also requires attending to many details ranging from professional development to laws and regulations a program must follow. Program policies and decisions work well if they flow from a vision of high-quality care and education as well as from ideas of family members, teachers, and other staff members. Program leaders strengthen everyone's commitment to work and learn together when the leaders set a respectful tone and ensure that all aspects of an infant/toddler program take into account the concerns and perspectives of family members, teachers, and other staff members.

Part Two: The Guidelines

This section presents two sets of guidelines: one for administering programs and one for facilitating early learning and development. Chapter 5, "Guidelines for Operating Infant/ Toddler Programs," applies to the entire program, providing relationship-based care and organizing the early care and education environment. The guidelines in Chapter 5 provide a sound basis for high-quality care and education. Addressing all policies and practices in Chapter 5 is necessary for effectively implementing the guidelines in Chapter 6. The second set of guidelines, Chapter 6, "Guidelines for Facilitating Learning and Development with Infants and Toddlers," focuses on particular domains or areas of infant/toddler development and also describes a curriculum process for infant care teachers.

Each guideline includes a rationale and suggested practices to help programs and teachers to attain the guideline. Every infant/toddler center and family child care home will have unique ways of achieving guidelines. The practices provide a starting place to help programs find ways to work toward each guideline. They are presented in categories so that recommendations on specific topics can be easily found. Many program leaders will recognize practices that they already have in place to provide high-quality care for infants and toddlers. Teachers and program leaders will be able to go beyond these recommendations as they use this publication to guide program improvement.

The guidelines set forth in this publication relate to the California Department of Education's (CDE's) Desired Results system. Many guidelines in chapters 5 and 6 contribute to the attainment of all six of the CDE's Desired Results. Some guidelines, particularly those in Chapter 6, focus only on learning and development Desired Results. Additional detailed information on these connections appears in the chart in Appendix C, which maps the links between guidelines and the Desired Results Developmental Profile-Revised.

All the guidelines together are intended to guide practitioners in the field toward continuous quality improvement that will support the complementary goals of high-quality care and the Desired Results system.

Guidelines for Operating Infant/Toddler Programs

"The . . . environment must be a space that welcomes the individual and the group, the action and the reflection. . . . [A]n infant toddler center is first of all a relational system where the children and the adults not only are formally initiated into an organization, a form of our culture, but also have the possibility to create culture. The creative act is much more possible when educational creativity involves not only the children, not only the teachers, but also the parents and the entire society around the children."

—C. Rinaldi, *Bambini: The Italian Approach to Infant/Toddler Care*

This section offers guidelines to program leaders and infant care teachers, including family child care providers,[1] as they create programs with families that support the learning and development of infants and toddlers in group-care settings. These guidelines rest upon the concepts presented in Part One. The development of family-oriented programs described in Chapter 1, the four insights into learning and development found in Chapter 2, and the roles of the infant care teacher and the program leader described in chapters 3 and 4 are represented throughout Chapter 5. This comprehensive perspective is essential. Every aspect of an early care and education program and everyone involved (infant care teachers, program leaders, family members, other children, and, when applicable, specialists) contribute to each child's learning and development.

This chapter focuses on the following topics:

1. Families
2. Relationships
3. Health and safety
4. Environment
5. Programs
6. Teachers

---

[1] These guidelines refer to family child care homes as programs and to family child care providers as teachers and program leaders. Any staff members who regularly interact with children are considered teachers as well.

Research and practice have demonstrated that following these guidelines leads to high-quality early care and education for infants, toddlers, and their families. By providing high-quality services, programs seek to achieve the CDE's Desired Results for Children and Families. The guidelines in Chapter 5 also provide an essential base for the learning and development guidelines in Chapter 6.

Providing *family-*oriented programs

Infant care teachers and program leaders create, together with families, relationships that foster the development and well-being of the child. To work effectively with families, teachers and program leaders must be aware of their own values and beliefs and must learn about those of the families they serve. This awareness is essential for clear communication and the development of positive relationships among program leaders, teachers, children, and their families.

1.1

Programs and teachers support the relationship between the family and the child as the primary relationship in a child's life.

The family is central in a child's life, for it is what the child knows. The child learns about himself and the world through experiences with his family. Families come in all forms and sizes. A single father may be the sole adult family member for his children. Another family may have several adult relatives, such as grandparents, aunts, uncles, and cousins, who are involved in raising a child. In this publication, *family member* is used to define the people who are primarily responsible for a child, including extended family members, teen parents, or foster families. Programs support the growth of the child within the context of the family by creating continuity between the home and the early care and education setting. Programs are responsible for learning about the child's home life through communication with family members and, when possible, home visits. As part of this process, programs will learn to work with diverse family structures, including those headed by grandparents, foster families, and teen parents. An essential aspect of high-quality programs is finding ways to support the growing relationship between the child and the family and adapting to the strengths and needs of each child–family relationship.[2]

PROGRAMS:

- Develop a written statement of philosophy or a handbook for families that emphasizes the importance of connecting the infant's experience at home with the early care and education setting.

Communication

- Let family members know that the program places priority on supporting the relationship between the family and the child.
- Share and discuss the written statement of philosophy with family members and adapt policies as needed in response to each family.

---

[2] The activities listed under "Programs" are carried out by the program leader working with teachers, other staff, and family members.

TEACHERS:

- Include the child and family members in the primary caregiving relationship (particularly in settings where families participate in the care of their children, such as programs serving teen parents).
- Make sure the presence of family members can be sensed by the child even when they are absent (such as by posting family photos or talking about family members).

Communication

- Offer family members frequent opportunities to explain how care is provided at home and to discuss their preferences so that they may be incorporated into care.
- Make time for informal and planned one-to-one meetings with family members as needed.

1.2

Programs and teachers are responsive to cultural and linguistic diversity.

From the moment families enter a family child care home or a child care center, they encounter culture in many ways. The noise level, voice tones, the language used, the colors, smells from the kitchen, and the ways in which children interact with adults and one another reflect the cultures of the families, teachers, and staff in the program. Program leaders and teachers need to convey to families through written, oral, and nonverbal communication that cultural and linguistic differences are honored and valued. Infant care teachers should work with families to create continuity between home and child care to help children feel comfortable and safe in the group-care setting.

Honoring diversity strengthens relationships with families and children, thereby enhancing the quality of care and education

Guidelines in this section link to the following Desired Results:

- DR 5. Families support their children's learning and development.
- DR 6. Families achieve their goals.

Children learn about themselves, others, and the world around them through their families. When teachers and family members communicate openly and regularly about each child, they can find ways to link the child's experience at home with her experience in the infant/toddler setting. The predictability that these linkages create for the child help her feel safe, loved, and understood in the program.

for infants and toddlers. When a child's home language differs from the language spoken most frequently in the program, teachers and families must work together to find ways to help the child feel comfortable and communicate his interests and needs in the group-care setting.

The structure of families also varies tremendously from family to family. For instance, a teen parent may reside with her parents, and the grandparents may be deeply involved in raising their grandchild and in participating in conferences with teachers and other program-related events. Acknowledging and respecting diversity among families gives an inclusive message and encourages families to participate in the program. A key way to acknowledge and respect diverse family structures is to provide intake forms that have additional space for the names of family members other than the child's mother and father to indicate their involvement with the child.

PROGRAMS:

- State in the philosophy statement or handbook the importance of connecting a child's cultural or linguistic experience at home with the early care and education setting.
- Develop outreach efforts to achieve representative staffing (culture, language, race and ethnicity, gender) at all staffing levels within the program.

- Hire infant care teachers who are representative of the children's cultural and linguistic communities.
- Encourage volunteers from the children's cultural and linguistic communities to participate in program activities.

Communication

- Invite extended family members to participate in program events.
- Provide program information and announcements in the home languages of the families.
- Provide an interpreter or someone representative of the family's culture, when necessary, to help in communication with the family.
- Initiate discussions with families about cultural preferences and practices and how these preferences may be incorporated into daily care and routines.

TEACHERS:

- Support a family's cultural style and respond positively to a child's expressions of cultural identity (for instance, a child may hug or kiss his father rather than wave "bye-bye").
- Reflect in interactions, play materials, family photos, room decorations, and celebrations the various backgrounds of the children in the program as well as other racial and ethnic groups in the community.
- Value the role of culture and home language in child-rearing practices and discuss their influence with families and other staff members.

Communication

- Speak a child's home language frequently or, if not fluent, learn simple, essential phrases of a child's home language and use them in daily communication with the child.
- Discuss with family members, on a regular basis, their children's care routines and other preferences and use this information to create continuity between home and the program.

- Acknowledge any tension that may arise over differing cultural practices and work with families to resolve or manage it.

Reflective Practice

- Find out if family members have similar or different assumptions about child-rearing practices.

- Participate in professional development activities that build awareness of one's own cultural beliefs and values about how children learn and develop and how best to nurture and teach them.

- Seek guidance from other professionals to support both other teachers and families when needed.

- Discuss culture and diversity issues with other care and education professionals in local networks or associations, particularly when working independently as a family child care provider.

1.3

Programs and teachers build relationships with families.

Programs convey an important message to families when they seek their views and collaborate with them in the care of their children. This message helps family members understand that their preferences and their concerns about the learning and development of their child are important to teachers and program leaders. When a teacher has open, honest, and understanding relationships with family members, the resulting links between the home and the early care and education setting often help their infant feel safe and comfortable.

PROGRAMS:

- Support the participation of all family members, being responsive to their cultural, linguistic, and economic differences, as well to as any disabilities or special needs of the children or a family member.

- Involve family members in making decisions about the program and its policies.

- Recognize and acknowledge that teen parents are still adolescents developmentally even though they are in an adult role as parents.

- Provide a way for families to give feedback to the program, such as regular evaluations or opportunities for informal discussion.

- Schedule regular meetings, social times, and other special events for families so that they can learn more about the program, get to know each other and staff members, and build a sense of community.

Communication

- Seek and consider families' views when identifying and hiring new staff members.

- Create an area for posting information for families (daily notices, outside services, child development information, community events, and job and education opportunities).

- Encourage communication between teachers and family members at the beginning and end of each day.

TEACHERS:

- Share a child's records with his or her family, including assessment information on the child's learning, experiences, and developmental progress.

- Learn about the different families in the program.

Communication

- Engage in a two-way exchange of ideas, preferences, and child-rearing philosophies during the first meetings with family members, setting the tone for future communication.

- Listen, reflect, and respond when family members communicate concerns and ideas about their child.

- Initiate discussions with families to understand and resolve issues when they arise.

- Engage in communication with family members at the beginning and end of each day about the child's care, activities, interests, and moods.

- Communicate to family members that they are always welcome to visit or call to check on their child.

Reflective Practice

Explore in discussions with family members both families' and teachers' assumptions about young children and how they learn.

Culturally Sensitive Care— A Way to Build Relationships with Families

"Acknowledge, Ask, and Adapt

By putting into practice the following steps for culturally responsive caregiving, you will gain the information you need to support appropriately the growth of all the children in your care.

Step 1: Acknowledge
The first step is a step of recognition in which you use your growing awareness of the existence of different cultural assumptions about infant and toddler development. A willingness to be open with yourself is essential to the success of this step.

Step 2: Ask
The second step is an information-gathering step. The goal is to get the information you need about the parents' and your cultural beliefs and values so that you can solve the problem together during the third step. Do not rush the second step.

Step 3: Adapt
In this last problem-solving step, you use the information gathered in step two to resolve conflicts caused by cultural differences and find the most effective way to support each child's growth."

—L. Derman-Sparks, "Developing Culturally Responsive Caregiving Practices: Acknowledge, Ask, and Adapt," in *Infant/Toddler Caregiving: A Guide to Culturally Sensitive Care*

Section 2

Providing *relationship-based care*

Guidelines in this section link to the following Desired Results:

- DR 1. Children are personally and socially competent.
- DR 2. Children are effective learners.

The development of infants and toddlers is enhanced when they have close, positive relationships. When programs implement the six policies and practices described in Chapter 4— responsive care, primary caregiving, small groups, culturally sensitive care, inclusive care, and continuity of care—the stage is set for children to develop positive and secure relationships with teachers. When a teacher is together with a small group of infants for a period of time, they have an opportunity to grow and learn together. Because the children stay together in a small group, they know one another intimately and are able to read cues, communicate, and predict each other's responses, which, in turn, creates a sense of safety and trust among the children. Because of his intimate experience with the group, a teacher can observe and anticipate the interests

of each child. In addition, when a teacher works with the same family over several years, the probability of better communication and collaboration grows. Collaboration with families is especially crucial for teachers who care for infants with disabilities or other special needs.

2.1

Programs and teachers provide intimate, relationship-based care for infants and toddlers.

Close, secure relationships support the development of a positive sense of self and provide the emotional and physical environment a child needs to explore and learn. In an intimate setting the teacher is able to appreciate and be responsive to each child's rhythms, temperament, interests, and needs, which supports the inclusion of *all* children. The policies of primary care, small groups, and continuity of care lay the groundwork for an intimate setting. Small family child care homes with one teacher have these relationship-based policies built into the program structure, which is a great benefit of this type of setting. However, like centers, both large and small family child care programs that

employ staff need to follow the policies of primary care, small groups, and continuity to ensure that the teachers and children have time and space for their relationships to develop. For all programs the policies of responsive care and education, culturally sensitive care and education, and inclusion of all children and families are essential components of relationship-based care.

PROGRAMS:

- Limit the size of groups so that teachers can provide close, caring relationships and easily adapt to individual children's strengths, abilities, interests, and needs.

- Provide staff members with professional development opportunities to increase their understanding of development and to support the implementation of continuity of care.

- Create policies and practices that ease transitions between the home and the infant/toddler setting as well as between settings when a child attends more than one program.

TEACHERS:

The program should have a "warming-in" process that allows the child and family members to get to know the teachers and the program gradually and allows teachers to learn about the child and family members by observing them together.

- Interact with infants in predictable ways.

- Follow a daily sequence of events so that infants can anticipate what is coming next.

- Maintain adult-to-child ratios that provide opportunities for one-to-one attention with each child throughout the day.

- Accommodate differing developmental levels and ages by adapting the environment and play materials as necessary.

Group Context

- Care for children in small groups in their own space separate from other small groups.

- Provide primary caregiving.

- Work as a team member with another primary caregiver or caregivers.

- Provide continuity of care in either same-age or mixed-age groups.

- Help children get to know a new teacher and build a trusting relationship with her if their current caregiver leaves the program.

- Help children and families who are new to the program and entering an established group get to know the other children and families.

Communication

- Communicate with family members about their child each day.

2.2

Programs and teachers ensure that all children have a sense of belonging.

For infants and toddlers to thrive in a group setting, a sense of belonging is essential. Belonging means full, unconditional membership in a group. An important part of belonging is a feeling that one's style and beliefs are respected and valued. All children have the right to be accepted and included for who they are. Children with disabilities or other special needs who are following a different developmental path benefit from a sense of belonging as much as any other child does. Belonging—feeling comfortable and connected to the early care and education setting and growing together with a small group of children—benefits everyone.

PROGRAMS:

- Comply with the Americans with Disabilities Act and care for children with disabilities or other special needs.

- Ensure that program materials—including handbooks, outreach information, and brochures—make it clear that families and children of all cultural backgrounds, home languages, and abilities are welcome in the program.

- Recruit and enroll children from diverse backgrounds and with diverse abilities.

- Include information in program materials for families about working with specialists who regularly visit to support children with disabilities or other special needs.

Child

- Provide appropriate support, accommodations, or adaptations so that every child may participate fully in the program.

- Celebrate and enjoy each child for the unique individual he or she is.

- Acknowledge and support a child's emerging abilities.

Communication

- Provide information to staff members about working closely with specialists who may be involved with a child or family.

- Provide opportunities for communication among the child's primary caregiver, other teachers, family members, and any specialists working with a child or family.

TEACHERS:

- Facilitate child-to-child interaction within the group and help children develop relationships with each other.

- Facilitate visits by specialists who support

"If I were the infant, would I like to be here?

Does the environment allow me to be able to do everything that I naturally would do?

Are there opportunities for me to anticipate what will happen next?

Is there a large enough and absolutely safe space in which I can move freely?

Is there a selection of safe and appropriate objects from which I can choose?

Am I given time to play without interruption?

Can I do what is expected of me?

If I cry, do I know the person who will respond?

If I am tired, do I have a peaceful place to sleep?

Does my caregiver observe closely in order to understand my needs?

Am I given time to work out my own conflicts as much as possible?

Does my caregiver give me full attention while caring for me?

Will my caregiver stay with me when I am a toddler?

Are my parents welcome to visit me at any time?"

—M. Gerber and others, *Dear Parent: Caring for Infants with Respect*

individual children with disabilities or other special needs.

Child

- Adapt to children's approaches to learning and interacting with people.
- Celebrate and enjoy each child for the unique individual she or he is.
- Work with families, other teachers, and specialists to create a plan for inclusion.
- Use information from specialists such as disability or mental health experts in providing service to all children, when applicable.

Reflective Practice

- Participate in professional conferences or activities to learn about working with children from diverse backgrounds or with disabilities or other special needs.
- Communicate with families, other teachers, and specialists about successes and challenges, observations, and reflections related to working with individual children.

2.3

Programs and teachers personalize care routines for infants and toddlers.

This guideline directly links to the following Desired Result:

- DR 4. Children are safe and healthy.

Personalized care begins with the relationships that a program and families build together. The family is the best source of information on how to care for the child and provide continuity between the home and the program. Personal care routines such as diapering, dressing, feeding and eating, or administering medication involve personal contact with the child. These times during the day provide a chance for the infant care teacher and the child to connect with each

other one-to-one. Each personal care routine provides an opportunity for a cooperative, communicative interaction. The teacher gains insight into the pace and abilities of the individual child as they work together to accomplish a task. The essence of personalized care is that a child receives the message that she is important, that her needs will be met, and that her choices, preferences, and interests will be respected. Following a child's unique rhythms and style promotes development of a positive sense of self and well-being and supports the child's growing ability to self-regulate.

PROGRAMS:

- Recognize personal care routines as key times during the day for emotional connections between children and teachers.

Communication

- Communicate to family members the importance of caregiving routines for teachers to develop and maintain relationships with each child in the group.

Group Context

- Support teachers as they organize daily caregiving routines that are adapted to each child.
- Support teachers as they strive for balance between the care of the individual child and the smooth functioning of the group.
- Support flexibility and collaboration among teachers so that other children in the group are attended to whenever their primary caregiver is occupied in caregiving routines with individual children.

TEACHERS:

- Approach personal care routines as opportunities for warm, cooperative interactions and communication.
- Understand and incorporate family preferences into personal care routines.
- Encourage children's participation in caregiving routines.
- Organize in advance the equipment and supplies needed for routines so that full attention can be given to the child.

Child

- Develop routines into rich, enjoyable experiences for each child.
- Follow individual mealtime and napping routines for children until they indicate that they would like to participate with others in the group.
- Follow individual diapering and toileting schedules for all children.
- Conduct routines in a predictable manner to allow the child to anticipate and cooperate during routines, but remain flexible and sensitive to changes in the child's mood or attentiveness.

Communication

- Minimize interrupting children to carry out personal care routines.
- Let children know in advance and assure them that, when an interruption is necessary, they can go back to what they were doing as soon as the routine is finished.
- Provide families with a record of their child's routines and activities for the day.

Section 3

Ensuring *health and safety*

Guidelines in this section link to the following Desired Result:

- DR 4. Children are safe and healthy.

Many teachers, including family child care providers, and program leaders have children of their own. They understand the act of trust that families show when they share the care of their child with others. Infants and toddlers are amazingly competent, but they still need adults to protect their health and well-being. Children also need to be safe in the relationships and the environments in which that competency develops.

Attending to emotional health and safety is as important for infants' well-being as is ensuring their physical health and safety. When children feel safe and loved, they can focus on the experiences around them that engage their curiosity and foster learning.

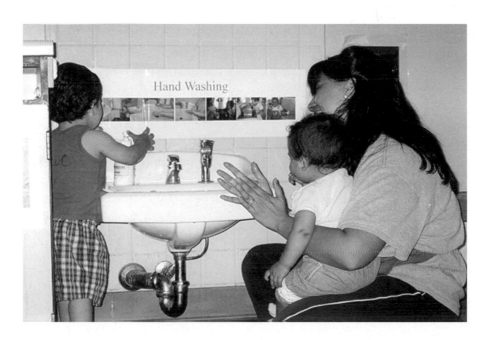

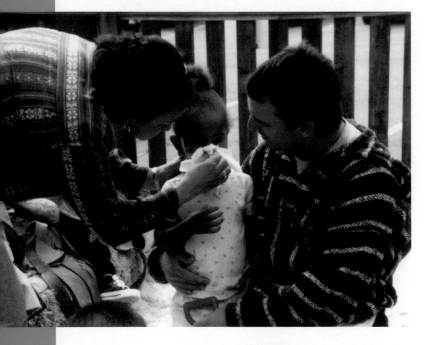

- Establish policies and procedures to administer medications reliably, safely, and in accordance with child care licensing requirements.

- Maintain high standards for cleanliness; for example, by emphasizing frequent hand-washing and washing and sanitizing of play materials, equipment, and surfaces.

- Seek community and financial support for health and safety improvements.

Communication

- Communicate with family members when children have been exposed to reportable communicable diseases or infestations such as chicken pox or head lice.

- Provide updates for staff members on current health issues and practices.

- Establish a relationship with a health care provider who can advise on good health and safety practices and who is sensitive to the cultural perspectives represented in the program.

- Maintain confidentiality when gathering information and communicating about the health of children.

Environment

- Make preparations for serving children with special health needs.

- Install classroom sinks and toilets, in centers, that children can use easily and that are convenient for teachers to supervise.

- Ensure that counters and sinks for food preparation are separate from and not used for diapering or toileting activities.

TEACHERS:

- Establish and follow procedures for maintaining good hygiene, especially during diapering and food preparation.

- Incorporate hand-washing and other hygienic activities into routines so that children can begin to learn healthy and safe habits early.

- Place infants in cribs on their backs when they are under six months of age or cannot easily turn over on their own, to lower the

3.1

Programs and teachers promote the physical health of all children.

Health is an important issue in all settings where children spend time and is especially critical in programs that care for groups of infants and toddlers. During the first months and years of life, children are particularly vulnerable to infectious disease, so proper hygiene and cleanliness are crucial to prevent the spread of illness. Low adult-to-child ratios and group sizes also play an important role in maintaining young children's health. For example, the risk of repeated ear infections increases in one- to six-year-old children who are cared for in groups of more than six children (Hardy and Fowler 1993). Research suggests that a ratio of fewer children per adult reduces the transmission of disease because caregivers are better able to monitor and promote healthy practices and behaviors (*Who Cares for America's Children* 1990).

PROGRAMS:

- Meet or exceed all required standards pertaining to health and nutrition.

- Maintain and update appropriate health policies and practices as well as health records and emergency contacts for all children.

risk of sudden infant death syndrome (SIDS), and communicate with families about this practice.

Environment

- Clean, maintain, and disinfect floors, surfaces, and all play materials regularly.
- Choose nontoxic cleaning supplies and classroom materials.
- Provide ventilation to ensure rooms have fresh, clean air.

3.2

Programs and teachers ensure the safety of all children.

Because infants and toddlers are competent and constantly on the move, program leaders and teachers must prepare the environment so that it is safe as well as interesting for children to explore. Programs must pay special attention to safety in infant and toddler programs because very young children are gaining new skills rapidly and they are continually testing their new abilities. Making safety a high priority helps family members to become confident that the teachers will protect their child in their absence and reinforces families' awareness of safety at home.

PROGRAMS:

- Maintain and update appropriate safety policies and practices.
- Prepare for emergencies and practice emergency procedures.
- Assign teachers to small groups of children so that children are continually supervised by someone who knows them well and can anticipate their behaviors.

Environment

- Ensure the program's facilities and indoor and outdoor play equipment meet or exceed safety standards for infant/toddler settings.

Best Practices for Preventing Disease

To help in preventing disease, early care and education programs should provide the following:

1. Information on immunization for all children and staff members
2. Identification and protection of children and staff members who are at high risk if exposed to infectious diseases
3. A systematic morning health check of children and staff members to exclude any individual who has an acute, contagious disease
4. Strict hand-washing policies, procedures, and training
5. Routine environmental cleaning and sanitizing practices
6. Strict universal precautions, policies, procedures, and training

Best Practices for Supporting Safety

To support safe practices, early care and education programs should provide the following:

1. Written policies and procedures relating to accident prevention
2. Periodic training for staff members on safety issues and accident prevention
3. An emergency plan and policies, procedures, and training to cover emergencies, such as fire, earthquake, or other natural disasters
4. An emergency care plan for each child
5. A general transportation plan and an emergency transportation plan
6. Staff members who are competent to assess an injury and to provide basic first aid and CPR
7. Consultants who can recommend environmental adaptations that will enhance the safety of all children, including children with special health care needs or disabilities
8. Periodic training regarding signs and symptoms of child abuse and neglect and reporting procedures
9. An incident, accident, and injury report form . . . for an injury log with specific information about the date and time of each accident, who was involved, what happened, who was notified, and what follow-up measures and steps were taken to prevent recurrence

—Adapted from B. Presler, California Institute on Human Services, *Health and Safety Considerations: Caring for Young Children with Exceptional Health Care Needs*

- Check all play equipment and materials frequently for safety and maintain and repair as needed.

- Provide adequate space for children to move without hurting themselves or others.

Communication

- Develop relationships with local firefighters, police, and other public safety officials to gain support in preparing for emergencies and to be assured of their assistance when needed.

TEACHERS:

- Continually monitor children of all ages to ensure they are safe even when they are sleeping.

- Anticipate and prevent safety problems (for example, remove toys from high-traffic areas).

Environment

- Arrange caregiving, play, and sleeping areas so that children can be seen and heard at all times.

- Ensure that children's areas are safe for exploration and free movement and are easily supervised, both indoors and outdoors.

- Select furnishings and play equipment (such as slides or ramps) that are both appropriately challenging and appropriately sized for the children in the group.

Communication

- Explain simple safety rules to older toddlers, helping them to understand and follow them.

3.3

Programs and teachers ensure that children are well nourished and that mealtimes support relationships.

Children's nutritional needs change as they develop and grow. In some cases the program provides meals; in others, family members bring their child's meals. Either way, close communication with family members about the child's daily nourishment is necessary to ensure a balanced diet for each child. How meals are provided is also important. Mealtimes can be wonderful opportunities for teachers to nurture their relationships with the children and also to support developing peer relationships. Holding young infants during feeding times offers teachers special one-on-one time with the child. Once children are able to sit in a chair while eating, they may start by

eating with one or two other children, eventually moving to a group setting. Eating together in a pleasant environment contributes to a sense of community, especially when mealtimes reflect the practices and preferences of the families. Mealtimes offer opportunities for teachers to support the development of healthful habits and attitudes toward food and help to ensure that children receive the nutrition they need to grow.

PROGRAMS:

- Support teachers as they work to adapt mealtimes to meet the individual needs of infants and toddlers.

- If the program provides food, follow recommended practices for well-balanced, nutritious, and developmentally appropriate meals that incorporate the food preferences of the children's families.

- Provide teachers with training and resources to incorporate nutrition education into daily experiences with toddlers.

- Provide the equipment or staff training necessary to enable children and adults with disabilities or other special needs to participate in mealtimes.

Environment

- Provide adequate space and facilities for mealtimes for all age groups.

- Provide a comfortable and private place for nursing mothers.

- Provide small tables and chairs for toddlers and infants who are ready to use them and comfortable chairs for adults when bottle-feeding infants and for sitting with children at the table.

Communication

- Invite family members who may wish to join children at mealtimes.

TEACHERS:

- Establish and follow procedures for proper preparation, handling, and storage of mother's milk, formula, and food.

- Provide individual mealtimes for infants and toddlers until toddlers begin to show interest in eating together in a small group.

- Hold infants on laps until infants are ready to sit independently at a child-sized table.

- Model healthful eating habits in front of the children.

Environment

- Use child-sized tables and chairs for mealtimes. Avoid use of high chairs or limit the use to mealtimes and ensure that footrests are adjusted.

Communication

- Sit and talk with children during meals (making sure everything needed for the meal is nearby to avoid leaving the table frequently).

- Talk with families to learn from them how to ensure consistent feeding practices between home and care.

3.4

Programs and teachers promote children's mental health.

A child's mental health is affected by social and emotional experiences; in particular, the emotional responses the child receives from other people. A child's mental health is inextricably linked to the mental health of the family members who are her primary attachment figures, whether they are parents, grandparents, or others. From the child's perspective, mental health is her sense of well-being: Does she feel safe and comfortable? Does she trust that her needs will be met? Social–emotional development and a child's progress in increasing self-regulation depend on the experience the child has in her personal relationships.

Programs that support infant mental health as a health and safety issue provide emotional as well as physical safety and security for infants and toddlers. A collaborative relationship with the family members helps program staff to understand the values that influence the family's interactions, expectations, and beliefs. Social–emotional well-being is necessary for a child to be mentally healthy. Infants and toddlers develop this sense of well-being in settings that reflect a clear understanding of the role that emotionally responsive and nurturing care and education play in a child's life.

PROGRAMS:

- Take steps to reduce staff turnover in the program to encourage positive relationships between infants and teachers and among teachers.
- Emphasize the importance of helping each child develop a sense of competence and importance.

Communication

- Maintain contacts with mental health professionals who can provide advice or services when children, family members, or staff members appear to be especially sad, under stress, unpredictable, or short-tempered over a period of time.
- Collect information on mental health services and offer referrals to families or staff members when appropriate.

TEACHERS:

- Observe and reflect upon children's emotional responses to the day's experiences and take these responses into consideration in all planning processes.
- Guide and support children's satisfying relationships with adults and peers.

Communication

- Discuss with family members children's interactions and emotional responses.
- Use a positive tone when responding to children's actions or words.

Reflective Practice

- Recognize the emotional nature of early care and education, taking time to reflect on one's own emotional responses (both positive and negative) to particular children, interactions, or events.
- Take a break or talk with a supervisor or colleague, when needed, to avoid immediately acting on difficult feelings.
- Seek help when experiencing mental health problems, such as depression or anxiety.

- Recognize cultural differences in understanding mentally healthy behavior.

3.5

Programs and teachers protect all children from abuse and neglect.

To protect children and prevent abuse and neglect, programs can offer support to families to help lessen the stress they may be experiencing. A positive relationship with the family opens the door for providing assistance. This support can come in the form of conversations, referrals to services, or information on education or job opportunities. In addition, program leaders can foster an environment in which teachers feel comfortable engaging in confidential discussions with designated staff members about concerns for a child and, as appropriate, with the child's family members. Program leaders and staff members must also understand and comply with requirements for reporting child abuse and neglect.

PROGRAMS:

- Develop program policies and practices to cover reporting (such as steps to take and with whom to communicate).

- Ensure that all staff members fully understand and comply with mandated reporting requirements.

- Seek the help of other professionals when necessary.

Communication

- Provide information to families on local services, physical and mental health care providers, and local job or education opportunities.

- Inform families of mandated requirements for reporting child abuse and neglect.

Reflective Practice

- Provide support to staff members who may experience stress associated with providing care for children whose behaviors may be erratic or difficult to handle because of abuse, neglect, or other trauma.

- Make sure that all teachers and other program staff members develop an

understanding of the difference between culturally distinct styles of caregiving, which may make a person feel uncomfortable, and abuse or neglect, which requires intervention.

TEACHERS:

- Observe each child carefully, noting clusters of behaviors or other signs that may indicate abuse or neglect.

- Understand and follow the state's mandated reporting requirements.

Communication

- Offer to talk with families about stress they may be experiencing; provide support and information or refer them to local resources when appropriate.

A Child's Sense of Self

"In effect, as parents we can allow our child in child care to miss us, but she should not miss herself. Her sense of herself, and of herself in relation to others, should not be damaged. That is the major loss in being separated from a good and adequate parent. Separation itself may be painful in many ways, but it pales in comparison with the child's loss of an effective, competent, well-loved self or a socially competent self who can relate and be related to. There must be relating partners who much of the time respond to a child as he is and in terms of his needs. There must be a sensitive, caregiving relationship, not mechanical caretaking."

—J. Pawl, "Infants in Child Care: Reflections on Experiences, Expectations and Relationships," *Zero to Three*

Section 4

Creating and maintaining *environments* for infants and toddlers

Guidelines in this section link to the following Desired Results:

- DR 1. Children are personally and socially competent.
- DR 2. Children are effective learners.
- DR 3. Children show physical and motor competencies.
- DR 4. Children are safe and healthy.

The space available to children and teachers plays an important role in the development of relationships within the program. In addition, a well-planned environment provides infants and toddlers with a space in which they can safely explore and learn. In both family child care homes and centers, the arrangement of space affects whether two children will be able to quietly flip through the pages of a book together or whether a child will be able to focus on the experiences that interest him.

Family child care homes are different from centers since the space used for care and education is usually also where the business owner's family lives (except where space is dedicated to child care, such as a converted garage). Family child care programs usually provide mixed-age care more frequently than centers do. The basic principles of high-quality environments apply to mixed-age groups in a home setting but may be put into practice in different ways. For instance, a couch may double as climbing equipment, and a bathtub may be a place to float boats in shallow water under the teacher's watchful eye.

The quality of the environment includes both the physical arrangement of the space and its emotional impact on children and teachers. Small-group sizes and low adult-to-child ratios contribute to a positive emotional climate. (See Tables 1 and 2.) To take full advantage of

Table 1. Recommended Ratios for Same-Age Groups

Age (Months)	Adult-to-Child Ratio	Total Size of Groups	Minimum Square Feet per Group
0–8	1:3	6	350
8–18	1:3	9	500
18–36	1:4	12	600

Table 2. Guidelines for Ratios in Mixed-Age Groups

Age (Months)	Adult-to-Child Ratio	Total Size of Groups	Minimum Square Feet per Group
0–36	1:4[a]	8	600

Note: In both tables the last column is based on minimum standards of usable square footage per child. The footage does not include entrances, hallways, cubbies, diapering, or napping areas.

[a]Of the four infants assigned to a caregiver, only two should be under twenty-four months of age (*Together in Care* 1992).

a small-group size and a low ratio, the environment must be well designed. An appropriate amount of space that is separate and sheltered from other groups enhances the ability of teachers and a small group of children to read one another's cues, communicate, build trust, and develop positive, nurturing relationships.

4.1

Both indoor and outdoor spaces support the development of a small community of families, teachers, and infants in which they build relationships of care and trust.

Young children and their teachers learn and thrive together in an indoor space that is large enough for the group, has comfortable furnishings for all children and adults, and allows an individual child or a small group of children to engage in quiet, focused play. These conditions increase the likelihood that children and adults will enjoy the environment together and that relationships and a sense of community will grow.

Effective use of outdoor space is essential for any program. When children can move freely between indoors and outdoors, their choices for exploration and learning are expanded. Even young infants benefit from being outdoors. Natural light, fresh air, and the sights and sounds of the outdoors contribute to good health, enjoyment, and togetherness for both children and adults.

PROGRAMS:

- Design the space with sufficient square footage per child to meet the needs of a small group of children. (See Tables 1 and 2.)

- Arrange the space so that family members feel welcomed and comfortable when they spend time at the program.

- Provide open space that can be rearranged to suit the current abilities, interests, and needs of the children to move freely.

- Create small, easily supervised play areas where infants can play alone or in groups of two to three without undue distraction from the sights and sounds of others.

- Design areas for care routines so that equipment and necessary supplies are conveniently located.

Group Size as a Health and Safety Issue

Research clearly demonstrates the importance of maintaining appropriate teacher-to-child ratios and group sizes. Teacher-to-child ratios and group sizes are two of the most frequent indicators of an infant/toddler program's overall quality and significantly affect many health and safety issues. Smaller group size is associated with a decreased risk of infection in group settings. The risk of illness in children between the ages of one and three years increases as the group size increases to four or more; whereas children in groups of three or fewer have no greater risk of illness than children cared for at home (Bartlett, Orton, and Turner 1986; Bell and others 1989).

Equipment

- Arrange furnishings and equipment so that adults can comfortably observe, supervise, and interact with infants.

- Include furnishings and display art and photos that reflect the home environments of the families in the program (such as wall hangings, hammocks, baskets, and pictures of family members).

4.2

The environment is safe and comfortable for all children, teachers, and family members.

Infants and toddlers spend many hours in care and education settings. The setting for them should become a home away from home. For teachers, other staff members, and children's family members, the family child care home or infant/toddler center should become a place of community and togetherness. Providing comfortable furnishings where teachers and children can relax together and creating an atmosphere that conveys both emotional and physical safety are essential for this type of setting. Program leaders need to keep in mind that what is comforting for one person may not be for another, and these differences tend to be deeply personal. For instance, a teacher may enjoy soft classical music in the background during routines, while some family members would prefer something a little more lively. When differences arise, two-way open conversations can lead the way to solutions. A comfortable and safe environment that everyone can enjoy contributes greatly to the quality of an infant/toddler program.

PROGRAMS:

- Ensure that areas and furnishings in the environment support full participation of all children and adults in the program, including persons with disabilities or other special needs.

- Provide a staff lounge, in centers, for relaxation and storage of personal belongings as well as for lunch and breaks.

- Provide a separate staff restroom, in centers, with adult-sized toilets and sinks.

- Play recorded music only when children show interest in listening to and playing with the music, not as a background sound.

Equipment

- Provide appropriately sized furniture and equipment that offer safety and comfort to children and adults.
- Provide equipment (such as a refrigerator, microwave oven, stove) for staff members to store and prepare meals.

Settings

- Provide several quiet, cozy areas that allow infants and adults to be together.
- Use light and color to create an effect that is pleasing, calming, and inviting.
- Select surface materials that are easy to clean and maintain and that support the intended use of each area.
- Use fabric and other sound-absorbing materials to reduce unwanted noise.

4.3

The environment is arranged and organized to support children's free movement.

Being able to move freely and spontaneously is essential for infants' exploration and discovery. When children are allowed to move in every way they are able to, they do so and change their positions frequently. They learn about themselves and the environment through movement and touch. Children are driven to move and feel great joy in moving freely. Children who are unable to move independently or who need support to move also learn from movement and exploration. Program leaders should turn to family members and specialists for guidance on appropriate ways to make adaptations in the environment to support physical and motor competence.

PROGRAMS:

- Provide ready access to the outdoors, with the possibility for children to move freely from indoors to outdoors.

Benefits of Well-Designed Environments

"The physical environment affects children's learning and development in many ways. Well-designed environments support exploration, give young children a sense of control, and enable children to engage in focused, self-directed play. . . .

The physical environment also affects relationships. Well-designed environments evoke a sense of security, which is a prerequisite in the formation of a healthy identity. And in appropriately designed classrooms, the children are given an opportunity to play both independently and in small groups, and the teachers are supported in their role as observers and facilitators of children's learning and development.

The physical environment affects a program's ability to promote best practices. It can become a tool for both staff and program development. An appropriately designed environment helps teachers to experience more appropriate interactions with children. Both indoor and outdoor spaces support the development of a small community, within which a small group of families, teachers, and infants build relationships of care and trust."

—L. Torelli, "Enhancing Development Through Classroom Design in Early Head Start: Meeting the Program Performance Standards and Best Practices," *Children and Families*

The Importance of Play

"As we observe infants, it almost looks as if they are working rather than playing: they are fully involved, absorbed in what they are doing. We don't need to invent exercises for them. They learn to follow their instincts and to trust their own judgment.

Infants accomplish mastery by endless repetitions, continuing the same activity over and over again, long after adults may have lost interest. When an infant repeats an action many, many times, he is not bored. Rather, he is learning thoroughly about that action, making it a part of himself and his world. When he has learned it to his own satisfaction, he will move on to another new activity.

While playing, children work through conflicts with objects, other children, and adults. Play provides an outlet for curiosity, information about the physical world, and a safe way to deal with anxiety and social relationships. In the long run, play serves children's inner needs, hopes, and aspirations."

—M. Gerber and others, *Caring for Infants with Respect*

- Provide play spaces that facilitate exploration and free movement for infants and toddlers, both indoors and outdoors.

- Arrange the play space to encourage exploration while minimizing the need for the teacher to say no.

- Arrange for alternative opportunities to move for children who have physical challenges.

Equipment

- Communicate with family members and specialists involved with the family about the proper use of adaptive equipment or alternative opportunities for movement for a child with a disability or other special needs.

- Avoid the use of restrictive equipment that limits children's free movement and isolates them from other children.

- Do not use walkers. In addition to being unsafe,

they have been found to interfere with the coordination of visual–motor skill development (Siegel and Burton 1999).

Settings

- Use dividers to create safe, protected play areas for infants who are not crawling or walking, both indoors and outdoors.

- Arrange walkways so that foot traffic of adults and children goes around, rather than through, children's play areas.

4.4

The environment is organized and prepared to support children's learning interests and focused exploration.

For infants and toddlers, every aspect of the world of people and things is interesting and engaging. When they are in a well-organized environment with clear choices, they easily find things that fascinate them and concentrate on learning. However, when an environment is disorganized or too stimulating, infants and toddlers may have difficulty focusing on any particular aspect of the environment. Programs and teachers must arrange the environment so that infants and toddlers can focus on the things that interest them. In addition, arranging the space so that infants are protected from the movement of older children lets everyone explore with confidence. Similarly, arranging play areas so that they are well defined and protected from traffic patterns lets toddlers play without interruption.

In family child care programs, areas are often defined by how the family uses them. For example, the kitchen is used for cooking and eating, or the living room or family room is arranged for the children's exploration and discovery. Areas for types of activity, such as a quiet area or an active area, can be set up within different rooms.

PROGRAMS:

- Create clearly designated areas for personal care routines by using furnishings that invite and support infants' involvement.

- Provide easy access to toys and materials by making them visible and available in wide, sturdy, attractive containers on the floor, low shelves, or elevated surfaces.

- Keep play areas inviting, organized, and safe, noticing when an area needs to be picked up (being careful not to interrupt children's play or take apart something on which they are still working).

- Allow children ample time to play within play areas without interrupting the play.

Equipment

- Provide children with ample play materials, giving the children interesting choices without overwhelming them.

- Provide enough equipment and materials, both indoors and outdoors, so that several children can engage simultaneously in the same activity.

- Offer toys and play materials found in the children's homes or communities.

Setting

- Create sheltered, quiet areas for exploration of toys and materials (such as books, puzzles, connecting and construction toys) that require listening and concentration.

- Provide predictable play areas, where children can reliably find familiar materials, and modify the environment in response to children's emerging interests.

Section 5

Engaging in *program* development and commitment to continuous improvement

Guidelines in this section link to the following Desired Results:

- DR 1. Children are personally and socially competent.
- DR 2. Children are effective learners.
- DR 3. Children show physical and motor competencies.
- DR 4. Children are safe and healthy.
- DR 5. Families support their children's learning and development.
- DR 6. Families achieve their goals.

Maintaining high-quality care and education for infants and toddlers is a continually evolving task. The program is always changing, taking in new children, new families, new teachers, and new leaders. As a result, the program needs to create a process of continuous review and improvement. Program leaders and teachers might ask the following relevant questions:

- How are we responsive to the infants, toddlers, and families we serve now?
- Where are the children in their development at this time, and how can we celebrate that?

- How else might we gain feedback from the families?
- How might we expand our resources and work together with our changing community?

Program development and improvement is not a one-time occurrence—it is a part of the climate that the program creates and maintains.

Family child care program leaders are in a unique position to shape the quality of care and education they provide. As small-business owners, they carry the major responsibility for improving the quality of their programs. By soliciting and responding to feedback from family members, mentors, and other teachers, family child care program leaders can assess how well their programs are serving children and families. With this information they can take steps to improve the quality of their programs and create care and education that is responsive to the community they serve.

5.1

Programs meet quality standards.

Programs are usually accountable for quality standards. Many programs (both child care centers and family child care homes) must meet requirements set by funding or regulatory agencies, such as Community Care Licensing in California. They may also be

required to document their effectiveness through a set of measures such as those that make up the CDE's Desired Results for Children and Families system. Frequently, programs on a path of continuous improvement and program excellence will choose another system of accountability, such as accreditation through the National Association for the Education of Young Children (NAEYC) or the National Association for Family Child Care (NAFCC).

The guidelines in this publication are not as specific as program standards. Many of the action points are similar to program standards, but the guidelines themselves present a broad goal that can be achieved in different ways based on the unique characteristics of a particular program. The guidelines are intended to be used in addition to program standards. Compliance with program standards represents an important part of implementing the guidelines set forth in this publication.

PROGRAMS:

- Meet or exceed all applicable program quality standards and regulations.
- Align program activities and assessments with the Desired Results system.
- Engage in continuous improvement, which may include becoming accredited by the NAEYC or NAFCC.

Communication

- Ensure that there is coordination with families and specialists for children who have individualized family service plans.
- Consult with families about the results of program evaluations.
- Discuss with families how to address problems or issues that are identified in a program evaluation.

5.2

Programs monitor the development of individual infants and toddlers.

Monitoring each child is an important way for programs to assess how well they are supporting children's learning and development. In California the Desired Results

Developmental Profile-Revised (DRDP-R) offers a carefully designed assessment tool for monitoring learning and development. Observations and assessments, combined with information from family members, allow program leaders and teachers to adapt care and education for the children and families currently enrolled in a program. The information on individual children also helps teachers and families consider whether a child should be referred for a formal assessment and evaluation by a developmental or medical specialist.

PROGRAMS:

- Gather information about a child through discussion with family members, observation of the child at different times, and reflection and discussion with other teachers.
- Involve family members in the ongoing assessment process.
- Conduct regular developmental screenings with each child, taking into account any cultural or linguistic limitations of the screening tool.
- Balance assessments across all the domains of development, using assessment tools such as the DRDP-R that reflect the full breadth of infants' and toddlers' development.

Communication

- Inform family members at the initial meeting that the program regularly documents children's development.
- Celebrate and support development, giving children many opportunities to enjoy the skills they are acquiring.

Reasons for Concern

"The child . . .

- By age three months, does not coo or smile.
- By age six months, does not babble to get attention.
- By age one, does not respond differently to words such as 'night night' or 'ball.'
- By age one, does not say words to name people or objects, such as 'mama' or 'bottle,' or shake head 'no.'
- By age two, does not point to or name objects or people to express wants or needs.
- By age two, does not use two-word phrases, such as 'want juice' or 'mama go.'
- By age three, does not try to say familiar rhymes or songs.
- By age three, cannot follow simple directions."

—From *Reasons for Concern That Your Child or a Child in Your Care May Need Special Help* (2004) (See Appendix E for the entire text.)

- Use a daily log to record notable events and to inform family members about the child's day as well as to record the child's feeding and eating, diapering or toileting, and nap routines.

Recordkeeping

- Maintain for each child a confidential file of all information required by licensing and other agencies.

Developmental Screening

At times programs may use screening tools. Programs and teachers need to understand what screening tools accomplish. Screening reveals one of two things:

1. The child is within the typical range of development at this time; or

2. The child needs further assessment.

Screening does not identify a definite delay nor does it guarantee that the child will not develop problems later.

Assessment and Evaluation

Assessment can be an informal process accomplished by gathering information and observation. Evaluation is generally a more formal process. Formal assessment and evaluation tools, such as the DRDP-R, must be completed by appropriately trained and qualified personnel. Assessment and evaluation include the following purposes:

1. To determine eligibility for services

2. To obtain a diagnosis (may be medical or educational)

3. To assist in program planning for the child

4. Any combination of the above (Brault 2003)

5.3

Programs engage in systematic self-assessment.

In high-quality programs leaders, families, teachers, and staff members collaboratively conduct ongoing reviews of program policies and practices in order to serve children and families as responsively and effectively as possible. Teachers and program leaders reflect regularly on their work with children and families. They use the insights they gain from reflection to create opportunities to expand children's experiences, learning, and development. Teachers communicate regularly with families to encourage their participation in the development of the care and education program. Through this process families learn that teachers and program leaders listen to and

value their ideas and incorporate their ideas in program development. Including families in collaborative self-assessment allows programs to align their policies and practices with the goals they set for children's care and education.

PROGRAMS:

- Assess on a regular basis how well the program is serving children and families.

- Use assessments to determine how well individual children's abilities, interests, and needs are being addressed and to strengthen planning.

Continuous Improvement

- Create systems for including the ideas and perspectives of everyone—families, teachers, staff members, and program leaders—in ongoing discussions of program development.

- Revise and adapt program policies and practices in response to a collaborative review and ideas from all program participants (families, teachers, and staff members).

- Implement changes respectfully, ensuring that everyone—teachers, staff members, and families—participates in the process and is aware of the changes that are occurring.

5.4

Programs develop and maintain partnerships within their community.

Family child care homes and infant/toddler centers are small communities that are linked to larger communities. When programs develop partnerships with community groups, such as social service organizations, other early care and education programs, local businesses, or volunteers, they strengthen their community connections. These connections, as well as participation in professional early care and education associations, may lead to opportunities to share resources, address common problems and issues that affect children and families, and expand the program's sense of community.

PROGRAMS:

- Build partnerships with other providers of early care and education in the local area.

- Develop and maintain lists or files of community resources that families can use.

- Develop policies and meaningful, appropriate roles for volunteers in the program.

- Welcome advice and support from outside service providers.

- Foster collaboration between teachers and outside specialists or consultants.

Communication

- Communicate with institutions of higher education about the participation of teachers in continuing professional development.

- Participate in the efforts of institutions of higher education to create appropriate learning opportunities for the early care and education field.

Outreach

- Initiate projects that help the surrounding community become aware of how children learn and develop and the services the program provides to the community.

- Create ongoing partnerships with community organizations, businesses, and agencies that are committed and able to contribute to children's well-being and learning through financial support, in-kind donations, or other resources.

- Join local, statewide, and national professional organizations, such as the NAEYC and NAFCC.

- Identify and work collaboratively with specialists in the community, such as health care providers, social service providers, and mental health professionals.

Section 6

Helping *teachers* continue to grow professionally

Guidelines in this section link to the following Desired Results:

- DR 1. Children are personally and socially competent.
- DR 2. Children are effective learners.
- DR 3. Children show physical and motor competencies.
- DR 4. Children are safe and healthy.

- DR 5. Families support their children's learning and development.
- DR 6. Families achieve their goals.

Providing care and education for infants and toddlers is an ongoing process that is dynamic, emotional, challenging, and personally rewarding. Teachers continually learn from the children, from the children's families, and from the community. Program leaders must support teachers' ongoing (informal and formal) learning, both as individuals and together as a group. A community that is based on respectful, collaborative relationships among adults also supports and celebrates the learning of all staff members. Just as fostering the growth of relationships among teachers, families, and children is important for children's development, fostering the growth of relationships between staff members is

important for the teachers' growth. The trust that grows from these relationships allows for the collaboration and creative problem solving necessary for teachers' professional development.

6.1

Programs hire well-qualified, representative staff members.

Programs that build a trained and educated staff are more likely to provide nurturing and enriching care to infants and toddlers. Hiring staff members who are educated and committed to the field of early care and education also lessens the likelihood of frequent staff turnover. Teachers appreciate when they work with colleagues who are knowledgeable and skillful. A professionally prepared staff creates a solid foundation for collaboration and continuous program improvement. Another consideration in hiring staff members is to seek to build a staff that is representative of the cultural, linguistic, and ethnic backgrounds of families in the program. A staff that includes individuals who are representative of the community is able to establish a high level of continuity between home and the infant/toddler setting. It also facilitates communication and understanding between the program and the families.

PROGRAMS:

- Hire a diverse staff, including teachers who are representative of the cultures, languages, and ethnicities of the families and children in the program.
- Seek teachers through community colleges' placement services and other organizations that support the growth of early care and education professionals.
- Encourage staff members to develop and maintain links with institutions that prepare early childhood teachers, including community colleges and universities.
- Establish high standards for qualifications of teachers.
- Work to ensure, when hiring and assigning staff members, that children experience

nurturing and responsive relationships with both men and women.

6.2

Programs create working conditions that support quality and job satisfaction to reduce turnover.

In a field where staff turnover is as high as 40 percent annually (Whitebook, Sakai, Gerber, and Howes 2001), finding ways to retain staff members is crucially important. Because research and experience so compellingly support the value of enduring relationships for infants, toddlers, and families, programs must make a strong commitment to staff stability. A climate of personal and professional support and respectful work relationships helps build a stable staff.

Family child care providers who employ staff members must address the turnover issue as well. For family child care providers who work alone, meeting with other providers regularly gives insights on how to make their job personally and professionally rewarding. Attending workshops, conferences, and college classes is a helpful way to develop relationships with colleagues and strengthen one's commitment to the field.

PROGRAMS:

- Identify resources in the community that could provide incentives to child care providers (such as free or reduced-price tickets to shows, free admission to community parks and museums, or discounts at stores).

- Schedule time and occasions for staff members to enjoy being together, such as dinners, retreats, or other social events.

- Arrange for on-call teachers to substitute for regular teachers when needed.

Reflective Practice

- Communicate respectfully with others at all times to promote responsive care and effective partnerships with other staff members and families and encourage inclusive classrooms.

- Acknowledge the emotional and physical demands on infant care teachers and respect their need for time to recharge.

Work Conditions

- Increase pay and benefits as teachers continue their education and professional development.

- Provide benefits for staff members, such as health insurance, dental insurance, vacation, and sick/family leave.

- Work with local and state government efforts to provide higher compensation for staff members.

6.3

Programs foster respectful, collaborative relationships among adults.

Respectful and collaborative relationships among adults lead to a strong, dynamic early care and education program. Every type of adult relationship—between teachers and other staff members in an infant center, between the family child care business owner and staff members, between families and

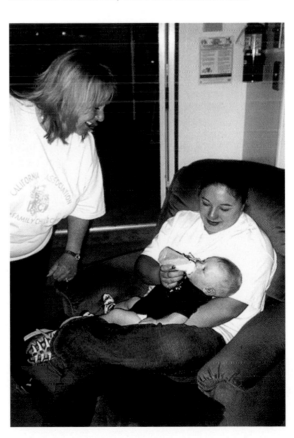

teachers, and between the families served—affects program quality. In shaping program policy and practice, leaders in centers and family child care homes need to respect and consider the values, beliefs, and expectations of all adults, including those of teen parents. Effective program leaders work to create continuity between a child's home and the infant/toddler program, facilitate the professional and personal growth of teachers, and model and foster respectful, collaborative relationships among adults. By allowing ample time for reflection and discussion, leaders ensure that the ideas of each participant are heard and considered in program development. This approach to leadership has a ripple effect throughout the program, strengthening respectful interactions between teachers and children.

Children are keenly aware of the feelings that adults have for each other and the behaviors the adults show toward each other. In other words they sense the quality of the relationships between their families and their teachers and among their teachers. They notice when the adults respect each other and cooperate, and children often imitate what they observe. Infants and toddlers are especially sensitive to the emotional tone of the teacher who is responsible for their primary care. When teachers are supported and feel appreciated, they become invested in their work and comfortable with each other, and the program becomes pleasant and inviting—a place where people want to be.

PROGRAMS:

- Model respectful interactions among adults.
- Support staff members' interactions with specialists involved with children or families.

Communication

- Talk with family members about how the program can adapt to meet their needs and goals.
- Communicate the value of respect in the staff handbook and family handbook and in all meetings.
- Provide ample opportunities for staff members to express their concerns and ideas.
- Understand that children are listening to conversations even when they are not directly involved.

Reflective Practice

- Create consistency between learning opportunities offered to family members and program practices—in particular, when parenting education is provided, such as in many programs that serve teen parent families.

Modeling Respect When Interacting with the Family Member and the Child

Fifteen-year-old Janea brings her infant daughter, Jade, into the classroom. Ruth, Jade's teacher as well as Janea's parent education teacher, smiles and says, "You did your hair differently, Janea—it's picture day at the high school, right?" Janea nods, looking shy. "My sister did it for me—we stayed up kind of late." Ruth nods and says, "Sounds like you and your sister had a sweet time creating a fun, new hairstyle for you."

Ruth greets Jade with a warm smile. Janea says to Jade, "Let's take off your jacket, Babygirl." Jade looks up as her mom tugs on the first sleeve. She gazes at her mom's face and raises her arm when Janea reaches for the next sleeve. Ruth smiles as she watches. "Janea," Ruth says, "When you tell Jade what you are doing like that she just lights up—it helps her to know what is going to happen. I think she feels included. What do you think?" Janea looks thoughtfully at her daughter and says to Ruth, "When I first came here and saw you talking to the babies, it seemed weird, but I guess I just got used to it. Jade seems to like it, and I love when she smiles at me." Janea kisses her baby's cheek. She goes on, "Sometimes people stare at me when I talk to her, like I'm crazy, but I really think she understands."

"I agree," says Ruth as she nods and turns to Jade. "Your mom and I are talking about how much you like it when she talks to you." Jade radiates happiness as both Janea and Ruth smile at her for a moment before Janea says bye and rushes off to class.

- Support teachers as they collaborate with family members and other staff members to solve problems creatively together.

- Address concerns that may arise among staff members, or between staff members and family members, using community resources and organizations if necessary.

6.4

Programs support the professional development and ethical conduct of infant care teachers and program leaders.

The development of individual staff members is necessary to promote high-quality care and education and appropriate standards of professional conduct. Access to ongoing professional development, geared to the characteristics and ages of children in the program, is a key to quality. Program leaders in centers and family child care homes need to support staff participation in professional development activities and the implementation of what staff members learn. Providing adequate compensation, with benefits and periodic pay increases, communicates to teachers that their contributions and hard work are valued. When staff members feel valued and respected, they are more likely to create environments that convey appreciation of others—including children, families, and colleagues. These environments, in turn, support families' participation in the program and children's healthy learning and development (Kagan and Cohen 1997).

PROGRAMS:

- Inform and consult with family members about continuing professional development activities for teachers and program leaders.

- Provide opportunities for teachers to participate in planning and decision making.

- Encourage staff to attend trainings or courses that cover the domains of infant/

A Professional Code of Ethics

"Ethical responsibilities to children. Our paramount responsibility is to provide safe, healthy, nurturing, and responsive settings for children. We are committed to support children's development; respect individual differences; help children learn to live and work cooperatively.

Ethical responsibilities to families. Because the family and the early childhood practitioner have a common interest in the child's welfare, we acknowledge a primary responsibility to bring about collaboration between the home and school in ways that enhance the child's development.

Ethical responsibilities to colleagues. In a caring, cooperative workplace, human dignity is respected, professional satisfaction is promoted, and positive relationships are modeled. Based upon our core values, our primary responsibility in this arena is to establish and maintain settings and relationships that support productive work and meet professional needs.

Ethical responsibilities to community and society. Our responsibilities to the community are to provide programs that meet its needs, to cooperate with agencies and professions that share responsibility for children, and to develop needed programs that are not currently available."

—From National Association for the Education of Young Children, *NAEYC Code of Ethical Conduct and Statement of Commitment* (See Appendix D)

toddler learning and development, elements of group care, children with disabilities or other special needs, influences of family, and curriculum.

Guidance

- Contribute to program improvement by creating and implementing a professional growth plan with staff.

- Present and help implement concepts and recommendations based on current research on early childhood development.
- Set clear expectations for professionalism and ethical behavior, such as those presented in the *NAEYC Code of Ethical Conduct*.

Support

- Provide professional development activities that relate to the infants, toddlers, and families who attend the program, including individuals with disabilities or other special needs.
- Provide adequate paid time and incentives for staff members to attend in-service training, classes, and conferences.
- Arrange for the program leader to engage in continuing professional development.

Teacher

- Shape a professional development plan with each teacher.
- Provide consistent opportunities for each teacher to meet with mentors, either within the program or through connections with other teachers.

- Provide professional development in the language or languages most easily understood by the teachers.

6.5

Programs use reflective supervision to support teachers.

Reflective supervision acknowledges that teachers are human, with emotions, personal histories, and beliefs that contribute to (and sometimes interfere with) effective teaching. Through regular, ongoing conversations, teachers and their supervisors explore together the many complex feelings, thoughts, and issues that arise in their work with children and families. In these conversations supervisors facilitate a process that offers needed support and helps teachers answer their own questions as they decide how to apply new insights and information to their everyday work with children and families.

In family child care the provider may not have a colleague or family member on site. In this situation providers benefit enormously from seeking support from other family child care providers in the community through meetings, phone calls, or even e-mails.

PROGRAMS:

- Provide regular opportunities for teachers to meet individually with their supervisor to reflect and plan.
- Set aside time during staff meetings for teachers to reflect on their practice.
- Observe teachers in their classrooms and engage in discussion with them about what occurred.
- Help individual staff members to reflect on their emotional responses to children, interactions, attitudes, and behaviors and to gain awareness of their own biases.
- Make time to reflect with other leaders in the early care and education community.

CHAPTER 6
Guidelines for Facilitating Learning and Development with Infants and Toddlers

By far the most important aspect of facilitating learning with infants and toddlers is understanding and responding to the fact that infants and toddlers are active, motivated learners. Infants and toddlers constantly explore the world around them, including people and relationships, and make sense of things based on their experiences and developmental abilities.

To facilitate means to make easier. Teachers who effectively facilitate learning make it easier for infants and toddlers to explore, concentrate on learning, make discoveries, and solve problems. Teachers can facilitate learning by creating situations that allow children to pursue their interests actively, observing as children learn, and expanding opportunities for learning. Teachers should begin by finding out about the children's interests and abilities from their families. Information from the families provides the foundation for observing children and being responsive to their inborn drive to learn and gain mastery. Effective teachers observe what children do in the setting, give them time for practice and repetition, communicate with children about their play and discoveries, and then offer suggestions to help children expand their exploration and experimentation.

The following guidelines are organized into two sections:

7. Facilitating Learning and Development

8. Implementing an Infant/Toddler Curriculum Process

The guidelines in this chapter describe how programs and teachers can facilitate learning and development by responding to infants and toddlers as active and self-motivated learners and by providing play and learning opportunities that honor and build upon children's abilities, interests, and learning styles. The curriculum process provides infant care teachers with an approach for extending and supporting the learning and development that occur naturally in a setting where children feel safe, connected to others, and free to explore. Above all this chapter also lays out a framework of professional development and content mastery for teachers to successfully facilitate the learning and development of infants and toddlers.

Understanding that *learning and development* are integrated across domains (physical, social–emotional, language and communication, and cognitive)

Guidelines in this section link to the following Desired Results:

- DR 1. Children are personally and socially competent.
- DR 2. Children are effective learners.
- DR 3. Children show physical and motor competencies.
- DR 4. Children are safe and healthy.
- DR 5. Families support their children's learning and development.
- DR 6. Families achieve their goals.

Infants and toddlers learn every waking moment. They continually learn about trust and security from their relationships. They learn about new ways to use things, discover social rules, and explore what is real and what is fantasy. For infants the areas or domains of development are not separate. Their learning and development in the physical, social–emotional, language and communication, and cognitive domains happen together and are integrated.

Teachers pursue professional development opportunities to better support the learning and development of infants and toddlers.

To respond to the daily challenges of care and education of infants and toddlers, infant care teachers need knowledge and an array of skills. To provide rich and meaningful learning experiences, teachers rely on their knowledge of infant learning and development, group-care issues and strategies, the children's families, and the unique characteristics of each child in their care. Infant care teachers have many options for continuing their professional

development, including college courses, training institutes, and in-service workshops. In addition, having a mentor or participating in a supervised practicum is a valuable way to continue professional development while on the job. (Program support and rewards for professional development efforts are essential and are outlined in Chapter 5, Section 6.)

TEACHERS:

- Find a colleague, supervisor, or another family child care provider who can be a mentor or a professional development adviser.

- Continue to pursue or create a professional development plan, which may include:
  - Enrolling in early childhood learning and development courses
  - Attending locally offered trainings
  - Participating in a supervised practicum
  - Participating in conferences
  - Creating a portfolio
  - Pursuing a degree in early childhood education

- Attend courses or trainings that cover the early learning and development curriculum areas outlined in Chapter 3 (page 28).

7.2

Programs and teachers facilitate learning across domains.

This guideline directly links to the following Desired Results:

- DR 1. Children are personally and socially competent.
- DR 2. Children are effective learners.
- DR 3. Children show physical and motor competencies.
- DR 4. Children are safe and healthy.

Infants and toddlers are constantly moving, thinking, communicating, and feeling. In other words they are learning all the time in many different and integrated ways. The way adults express emotions, the tone of voice they use, the pace of the personal care routines, the materials provided for discovery, even the quality of light in the environment all contribute to the children's construction of knowledge. Because their learning is integrated across domains and is occurring every moment, infants learn during play as well as during caregiving routines. In essence, teachers' actions and emotions communicate to children even when children are not directly involved in an interaction.

Understanding that children learn and develop in an integrated way leads to such questions as "What captures this child's interest?" or "What is she discovering as she explores these materials?" Young children repeatedly demonstrate to teachers their amazing capacity to learn. An essential role of the teacher is to support and guide children's interests in a manner that engages their natural enthusiasm and energy for exploration, repetition, and discovery. Infant care teachers need to be aware of the diverse ways that all children, including

Physical and motor, social-emotional, language, and cognitive learning all happen together

Asha grasps the rounded edge of the coffee table with both hands and pulls herself to standing. She smiles at Erica, who is sitting on the couch giving a bottle to Orlando. Asha points to Orlando and nods. Erica says, "Orlando is having his milk. You just had your milk a little while ago." Asha nods again. "Mmm," she says with effort. Erica responds by saying, "Yes, Asha, milk, milk in a bottle." Asha carefully lowers herself to the floor saying, "Baah . . . baah." She crawls around the table and pulls herself up holding on to Erica's knee. Asha points so closely to Orlando that she accidentally pokes his cheek. He starts to cry, but then he decides to go back to sucking on his bottle. He watches Asha closely. Erica strokes both Orlando's cheek and Asha's cheek and says, "Oops! Asha poked Orlando's cheek. Asha, were you pointing to the bottle?" Asha looks at Erica with wide eyes and says, "Baah baah."

those with disabilities or other special needs, explore, experiment, and learn. For example, some children may observe or listen a good while before acting; others may immediately reach out to touch and handle a new object. Or some children may want to share each discovery with an adult, and others may choose to explore and make discoveries on their own. Teachers who appreciate these differences become able to support learning as it occurs in the context of each child's daily experiences.

Because learning is integrated for infants and toddlers, whatever an infant care teacher does with the children is related to all the Desired Results. Likewise, teachers observe each child's progress in all the developmental domains at the same time. The Desired Results Developmental Profile-Revised (DRDP-R) indicators help teachers focus on specific areas while the child is learning in multiple domains. For example, when trying out a new motor skill, a child may also be learning language, developing problem-solving skills, and learning rules for social behavior.

PROGRAMS:

- Communicate with families about an integrated approach to facilitating learning.
- Understand that daily interactions and experiences influence all areas of development.
- Avoid the use of television, video players, computers, and other electronic devices in infant and toddler care.

Support

- Support teachers in providing a variety of learning experiences related to children's interests and abilities.
- Provide training and professional development for teachers about the integrated nature of learning in early childhood.

TEACHERS:

- Communicate regularly with families about children's learning (using, for example, newsletters, notes sent home, documentation posted on walls, video tapes, audio tapes, photographs with explanations attached, and so on).
- Provide a variety of developmentally appropriate materials for infants and toddlers that are easily accessible and available throughout the day.
- Adapt environments as children's interests and abilities change.
- Approach caregiving routines as opportunities for infants and toddlers to learn in all domains of development.

Orientation

- Allow all children time to observe and explore freely at their own pace objects, ideas, or actions that interest them.
- Understand the importance of practice and repetition in learning.
- Maintain a strong connection to what is familiar to the child when providing new materials or opportunities for learning.
- Remember that children are careful observers and that teachers are models of behavior even when they are not trying to be models.

Interaction

- Follow a child's lead, allowing infants and toddlers to choose activities and play materials in the play environment.
- Participate in spontaneous group activities as they occur.
- Encourage further exploration, experimentation, and creativity by watching, waiting, and commenting on what children are doing.

- Observe a child solve a problem or make a discovery, remain available, but allow the child to decide what happens next.
- Avoid interrupting a child who is concentrating—observe and wait for an appropriate moment.

7.3

Programs and teachers facilitate physical development and learning.

This guideline directly links to the following Desired Result:

- DR 3. Children show physical and motor competencies.

Physical development consists of a variety of reflex movements at first and gradually becomes increasingly purposeful and coordinated. All infants and toddlers continually learn about themselves, their environment, and other children and adults when they move freely. They experiment and make discoveries about weight, gravity, textures, balance, what moves and what does not, and what fits and what does not. Infants and toddlers use their large or gross muscles (such as those that control the arms, legs, and trunk) as well as their small or fine muscles (such as those that control eye movements, fingers, or toes). Children with delays in their motor development will generally progress through the same stages but at a slower pace; some may follow a different developmental path.

Teachers and programs effectively facilitate physical development by recognizing that gross muscle movements (such as in rolling, crawling, climbing, moving heavy objects) are just as important in learning as are small-muscle movements.

PROGRAMS:

- Create an environment that is safe for free movement and exploration.
- Create physical boundaries to keep children from entering unsafe places (such as a bathroom) unattended.

Equipment

- Provide a variety of developmentally appropriate play equipment that offer opportunities for large-muscle movement both indoors and outdoors.
- Provide a variety of objects and materials for children to explore with their small muscles.

TEACHERS:

- Adapt the environment so that all children can move freely in accordance with their own abilities and interests.
- Allow infants who are not crawling or walking to move freely in a space where they are protected from more active infants or older children.

Interaction

- Provide opportunities for both indoor and outdoor experiences for all children.
- Remain available to infants and toddlers as they physically explore the environment.
- Give children time to solve problems they encounter as they experiment with large- and small-muscle movements.

tions, needs, and interests. Experiences in relationships with others affect the child's emerging sense of identity and feelings of security. At the same time, interacting with others influences the child's intellectual, language and communication, and physical development. Infants who become emotionally secure through nurturing relationships freely explore their environment and become confident learners.

PROGRAMS:

Implement policies and support practices for relationship-based care.

TEACHERS:

- Observe and respond to infants' verbal and nonverbal cues.
- Respond to crying by giving full, sensitive attention, speaking in comforting tones, and holding to soothe, as appropriate.
- Provide enough predictability, without adhering to a rigid schedule, that children can anticipate interactions and events.
- Enjoy opportunities for one-to-one interaction as they occur throughout the day.
- Allow authentic expression of feelings by offering support and comfort rather than distracting the child.
- Remain available during greetings and departures, which can be vulnerable times for children and family members.

7.4

Programs and teachers facilitate social–emotional development and learning.

This guideline directly links to the following Desired Result:

- DR 1. Children are personally and socially competent.

Research and experience have repeatedly shown that personal and social competence are closely linked to all other domains. As infants and toddlers interact with others, they learn about themselves and others. In particular, they learn how others respond to their emo-

The Developing Infant

"An infant's first learning occurs in an interesting personal, emotional, and social interaction. That learning is certainly about how someone smells, sounds, looks, and feels; it is also about how one engages this other person, how one regulates oneself and each other, how one learns to capture and maintain each other's attention as well as how each imitates and anticipates the other. The baby learns to share feelings, to intensify or

dampen them, and this is learned in tandem. The developing infant becomes interested in the objects enlivened by a partner; she is endlessly curious and begins to explore places and things on her own in the security of the relationship. Gradually, different feelings are sorted and she learns how to soothe and quiet herself with maybe just a touch, or a look, or a word . . . or maybe not, depending on who she is to begin with. Children master these things at different rates and

need different things to help them along. They also are more or less shy, bold, intense, distractible, and eager to please. Learning the individual emotional characteristics of each child is interesting and necessary if one is to be genuinely and usefully responsive. Finding the special ways which each growing infant and toddler best responds is a great part of the pleasure."

— J. Pawl, Guidelines Expert Panel member

Socialization

- Provide guidance to infants and toddlers as they learn how to be with each other and with the larger community (children from other classrooms, staff members, volunteers, and other children's families).

- Help children understand the beginnings of social behavior. ("You offered her the doll, and she took it. Now she is offering you a doll. You made a trade. How thoughtful!")

- Model respectful relationships by avoiding communicating concerns about a child in the presence of children.

7.5

Programs and teachers provide guidance for social behavior.

This guideline directly links to the following Desired Result:

- DR 1. Children are personally and socially competent.

One of the most challenging and rewarding aspects of infant/toddler care and education is that of guiding behavior and facilitating socialization. Infants and toddlers in groups develop close, emotional relationships with each other. From the first, infants and toddlers are interested in other people. Many families and teachers have been surprised to find that even very young children are aware when someone is absent or feeling sad. Infants and toddlers gradually respond to the thoughts and feelings of the people around them. They learn about how their own actions influence other people. They discover the difference between interacting with adults and with other children. Because infants and toddlers learn from both interacting with people and watching others interact, adults in early care and education settings need to interact respectfully with each other as well as with children.

When conflicts arise, teachers help infants and toddlers learn ways of managing intense emotions without hurting other people. Young children look to adults they trust to set limits for them and guide their behavior. One of the most important ways that teachers foster socialization is to set up calm, safe environ-

ments for small groups of children. A well-planned program can prevent conflicts between children and encourage them to engage in positive interactions with each other.

PROGRAMS:

- Communicate with family members about the program's socialization and guidance policies and practices, seeking views from each family about their child.

- Implement continuity of care so that groups of children and teachers know and can anticipate each other's behavior.

TEACHERS:

- Prepare the environment to encourage smooth group interactions (for example, provide enough play materials for all children to be engaged; arrange play areas to encourage small, focused groups of children).

Playing in Water

Elio and Sandi were gleefully dropping blocks in the toilet while their teacher, Juan, was changing another child's diaper. They giggled and looked at each other when the blocks made a plopping sound.

A moment later, when Juan saw what was happening, he realized that he had left the gate between the play area and the bathroom unlatched. Juan kneeled down and said, "This is not a place for playing. I can see that you like playing in water, but this is not the place." Juan helped the two toddlers wash their hands thoroughly. Elio protested loudly and reached over toward the toilet—he was not finished with the game! Juan listened to him and said, with empathy in his voice, "Yes, you really liked that game. I will find another way for you to play in water." Elio was not happy about it; he cried and resisted Juan's attempt to hold him.

Then Juan placed some tubs of water on the water and sand table and observed as Elio and two other children found items from the play yard to drop into the water.

Reciprocal Interaction

"The back-and-forth emotional interaction in making sounds leads to more vocalizations, the meaningful use of sounds, and, eventually, the meaningful use of language. An example of this back-and-forth (or reciprocal) interaction is when a child vocalizes for her rattle or to get a smile and receives a purposeful response, such as getting her rattle or a smile from her teacher. When interactions like this occur again and again, the child learns that these utterances are useful tools. As a result, she will be more and more likely to explore her developing language."

—S. Greenspan, Guidelines Expert Panel member

- Interact respectfully with infants and toddlers, both emotionally and physically.
- Guide behavior in ways that take into account each child's developmental abilities.
- Model appropriate behavior and remain an active presence to prevent problematic situations.

Orientation

- Approach guidance by understanding that the child is a competent problem solver trying to negotiate a complicated social world.
- Remain aware of individual differences in children's ability to tolerate frustration or deal with stress.

Addressing Concerns

- Understand that exploratory behaviors, such as testing limits and making mistakes, are some of the ways infants learn and that sometimes they may need redirection. (See "Playing in Water" on p. 93.)
- Intervene when children are about to cause harm to others or the environment.

- Explore with a child's family possible causes of stress or changes in behaviors.
- Work together with families to develop ways to guide, without creating or reinforcing a negative self-image, children who exhibit challenging behaviors.
- Acknowledge a child's angry feelings with a gentle response (being sensitive to differences in the expression of emotion) and, if necessary, redirect the child's behavior.

7.6

Programs and teachers facilitate language and communication development and learning.

This guideline directly links to the following Desired Result:

- DR 1. Children are personally and socially competent.

From the start, young children seek to communicate with others. Infants learn about the power of communication from adults' responses to their first attempts to communicate with gestures, facial expressions, and sounds. Infants need adults to communicate nonverbally and verbally with them. These early experiences with communication lay the foundation for learning language and are important first steps in preliteracy development.

For infants whose language at home is different from the language their teachers speak, supporting the development of both languages is critically important. Having competence in the home language assists children in identity development and communication with family members. In addition, children who gain mastery in two languages during the early childhood years have a strong basis for learning to read in elementary school. Their rich understanding of language through learning English and their home language contributes to their continued literacy development as they grow older.

PROGRAMS:

- Support teachers as they take time to listen and respond to infants and toddlers in their care.

- Encourage discussion between teachers and family members about children's language and communication development and learning.
- Hire teachers who speak the children's home language, if possible.
- Provide numerous and varied opportunities for children whose home language is different from English to experience their home language in the care setting. For example, volunteers from the community can regularly visit and tell stories, read books, and sing songs in the child's home language. Tapes and books in the child's home language also support bilingual development.

TEACHERS:

- Converse regularly with families about children's verbal and nonverbal communication (for example, "Sanjay said 'baba' over and over this morning during breakfast. What do you think he meant?").
- Respond to children's verbal and nonverbal communication.
- Respond positively to children when they communicate in their home language.
- Encourage children whose language at home is different from English to continue developing their home language.

- Talk to infants and toddlers in a pleasant, soothing voice, using simple language and giving children ample time to respond.

Child-Initiated Communication

- Repeat words, sounds, and hand gestures that children use to communicate and wait for a response.
- Pay close attention to the gestures of babies with a family member who is deaf, as these babies may "babble" with their hands.
- Respond to children when they practice and play with language.

Volunteers Make a Difference

In one community men from all corners of the community volunteered to go into child care programs once a week and read books, tell stories, or sing to children. Some of the men were fathers or grandfathers, and others were not.

In many cases the men were released from work to read to the children, and afterwards they returned to their jobs. They arrived with books under their arms, wearing tool belts and hard hats or business suits. They read to children in their home languages. Some of the men told stories from their communities' oral tradition, complete with voice variation and gestures. Others sang songs they remembered from childhood. They laughed when their voices cracked, and the children did not mind one bit. In fact, the children did not mind when a song or story was in a language they had not previously heard. They appeared to enjoy the experience anyway.

The volunteers found that the children liked hearing the same simple songs and stories over and over. They also learned that a small group of two or three very young children may sit for a story, and then one may leave, and a little later another may join the group. Although the situation kept changing, the men had a lot of fun. They donated books to the child care centers and family child care homes they visited. The children, the teachers, the family members, and the volunteers all enjoyed these weekly visits.

- Give children many opportunities to express and explore their unique qualities, interests, and abilities.

Teacher-Initiated Communication

- Ask simple, open-ended questions related to children's interests and wait for a response.
- Comment on a child's focus of interest or activity.
- Describe objects, events, interactions, behaviors, and feelings as children experience them during the course of daily routines and other activities.
- Listen and add to topics toddlers initiate, encouraging give-and-take communication.

Programs and teachers nurture a love of books and stories.

This guideline directly links to the following Desired Results:

- DR 1. Children are personally and socially competent.
- DR 2. Children are effective learners.

The foundation of literacy is established in the early years through a variety of two-way exchanges with others, such as pretend play, imitation, songs, and experiences with books and stories. Seeing teachers appreciate and use books heightens young children's fascination with books. Reading with infants and toddlers is an important way to introduce them to books and the written word. A warm lap, an exciting story, and a quiet time with a responsive teacher motivate young children to seek out reading opportunities. Children often are especially interested in books and stories that contain themes and pictures that relate to their lives. For instance, many teachers and family members know that young children are fascinated with stories of a mother looking for her baby. There are numerous versions of this type of story all around the world. Young children are also drawn to books that feature pictures of people who look like them and their family members. Photo albums that tell stories of the children and their families or events in child care are a wonderful way to help children recall and reflect upon experiences.

Discovering Books Together

Eighteen-month-old Ricardo walks over to the book corner as he keeps his left hand moving along a low toy shelf leading to the book corner. His teacher, Rosa, is seated comfortably on a large beanbag holding another child, who is thumbing through a cloth book in her lap. Rosa watches Ricardo to make sure he navigates his way to the book area safely. Ricardo smiles when

he bends down and feels the edge of the beanbag and Rosa's leg and hears her voice: "I'm happy that you could join us, Ricardo."

Rosa has added a couple of textured and sound books to the book corner with Ricardo in mind, since he has a visual impairment. Rosa knows that the other children in her care will also benefit from reading and exploring these books. "Doggie,"

says Ricardo, as he hands to Rosa the textured book of animals he picked out. He knows the book and finds it each time he enters the book corner.

Rosa reaches for the book and accommodates Ricardo on her lap along with the other child. As she guides each child to turn the pages, Rosa also guides them to feel the texture as she names each animal.

In high-quality settings storytelling is also a valued part of the program. Storytelling has a long and rich history. Family members and volunteers from the community may be able to contribute to the children's learning by visiting the program and telling stories.

PROGRAMS:

- Communicate with families to learn about which books and stories are important in the home and find ways to bring those books into the program.

Books

- Provide a variety of books and pictures that are sturdy enough for children to handle on their own.
- Ensure that children's books are developmentally appropriate.

TEACHERS:

- Offer opportunities for playfulness with language.

Books

- Encourage children's free exploration of books.
- Look at books with children; read to them and tell stories when they are interested.
- Read or describe pictures to infants, when they show interest, so that they can enjoy the pictures, the rhythms of the text, and the sound or feel of the pages turning.

Stories

- Learn finger play, songs, and simple games from each family.
- Participate playfully as toddlers engage in activities that involve self-expression, such as make-believe and dramatic play.

7.8

Programs and teachers facilitate cognitive development.

This guideline directly links to the following Desired Result:

- DR 2. Children are effective learners.

Infants learn through exploration and imitation. Intellectual activity in infants and

toddlers is driven by the child's inborn curiosity and motivation to understand the world and share meaning with others. Through following their own play interests, children make discoveries about gravity, relative size, quantity, or the use of tools. (See box on page 97.)

Infants explore through their senses and through movement. For instance, infants' mouthing and banging inform them about the properties of objects. As infants grow older, their ways of exploring become increasingly sophisticated and complex. Infants who mouthed and randomly banged objects begin to experiment with the different sounds of objects banged on different surfaces. Through exploration and experimentation infants and toddlers learn about the relationship between cause and effect, for example, and how things move and fit in space.

Infants and toddlers constantly watch the behavior of adults and other children, wanting to be like others and do what they do. Teachers and family members see their actions reflected in children's social behavior and handling of objects. For instance, a young toddler may hold a toy phone to his ear with his shoulder, as he has seen a family member do at home.

The teacher's role in facilitating cognitive learning and development is to understand the child's stage of development and to use this understanding when setting up the environment, selecting materials, and planning interactions to encourage and expand the child's learning. When teachers understand

that young children's play is rich in discovery and learning, they find ways to support, facilitate, and extend children's playful exploration of the world.

PROGRAMS:

- Work closely with family members, teachers, and specialists to facilitate cognitive competence in children with disabilities or other special needs. For many children with delays in cognitive development, learning is best accomplished through active experience and ample opportunities for repetition and practice.

Materials

- Make available board books, materials that change shape when manipulated, and things that fit together (such as nontoxic play dough, soft blocks, nesting cups).
- Provide materials that give children opportunities to learn about cause and effect, relative size, number, quantity, and grouping.
- Provide materials that support children's interest in imitating others (such as toy phones, dolls, objects from home).

TEACHERS:

- Observe to understand the focus of an infant's attention.
- Rotate toys, both inside and outside, when children have not used them for a while.
- Allow children to engage freely in exploration even if over a long period of time.
- Remain flexible and adapt to a child's creative ways of manipulating or exploring materials (for example, a child puts a handbag on his head as a hat).

Orientation

- Let children's interests be your guide to facilitating cognitive development.
- Recognize that what the child chooses to do is the most important thing for the child to be doing at that moment.
- Acknowledge when a child has a mastery experience, in other words has accomplished something and feels good about it.
- Pay attention to a child's growing ability to remember or to hold images in her mind (for example, when an older toddler talks about a loud trash truck she heard at home that morning).

Assistance

- Wait and watch before helping a child engaged in exploration. Assistance given too quickly might interrupt a significant learning experience.

- When a child asks for help, provide only the assistance requested by the child and do not take over. Help a bit, in the context of the learning situation.

Discoveries of Infancy

"Learning Schemes

Learning schemes are the building blocks for all other discovery during infancy. By using schemes such as banging, reaching, and mouthing, children gain valuable information about things. Scheme development helps children discover how objects are best used and how to use objects in new and interesting ways.

Cause and Effect

As infants develop, they begin to understand that events and outcomes are caused. They learn that:

- They can cause things to happen either with their own bodies or through their own actions.
- Other people and objects can cause things to happen.
- Specific parts of objects, for example, wheels, light switches, knobs, and buttons on cameras, can cause specific effects.

Use of Tools

Tools are anything children can use to accomplish what they want. Among the tools infants use are a cry, a hand, a caregiver, and an object. Infants learn to extend their power through the use of tools. They learn that a tool is a means to an end.

Object Permanence

For young infants, 'out of sight' often means 'out of mind.' Infants are not born knowing about the permanence of objects. They make this important discovery gradually through repeated experiences with the same objects, such as a bottle, and the same persons, such as their mother or father. Infants learn that things exist even when one cannot see them.

Understanding Space

Much of early learning has to do with issues of distance, movement, and perspective. Infants learn about spatial relationships through bumping into things, squeezing into tight spaces, and seeing things from different angles. In a sense, infants and toddlers at play are young scientists, busily investigating the physical universe. For example, they find out about:

- Relative size as they try to fit an object into a container
- Gravity as they watch play cars speedily roll down a slide
- Balance as they try to stack things of different shapes and sizes

Imitation

One of the most powerful learning devices infants and toddlers use is imitation. It fosters the development of communication and a broad range of other skills.

Even very young infants learn from trying to match other people's actions. . . .

As infants develop, their imitations become increasingly complex and purposeful. . . . At every stage of infancy, children repeat and practice what they see. By doing the same thing over and over again they make it their own."

—*Discoveries of Infancy: Cognitive Development and Learning* (PITC Child Care Video Magazine)

Implementing an infant/toddler *curriculum* process

Guidelines in this section link to the following Desired Results:

- DR 1. Children are personally and socially competent.
- DR 2. Children are effective learners.
- DR 3. Children show physical and motor competencies.
- DR 4. Children are safe and healthy.

As active learners infants and toddlers have their own curriculum that teachers can support and strengthen. Infants and toddlers are engaged in learning about themselves and the world around them in many different ways.

Effective teachers use a curriculum process that is responsive to infants' and toddlers' interests and abilities. Program leaders play an important role in supporting teachers as they facilitate children's learning and development. The following guidelines describe the teacher as one who continually learns and adapts to meet the learning agenda of infants and toddlers as individuals and as members of a group.

The infant care teacher has the responsibility to observe, document, and assess each child's developmental progress. Because the California Department of Education's DRDP-R is based on naturalistic observation and a developmental conceptual framework, it is presented in this publication as an integral part of the curriculum process. The DRDP-R is considered key in planning for individual children. Rather than being two separate documentation activities, the curriculum process and the DRDP-R work hand in hand to help infant care teachers facilitate the learning and development of infants and toddlers.

8.1

Teachers observe children during personal care routines, interactions, and play.

Through observation the teacher gets to know each infant. Observing each child helps the teacher make decisions about how to support learning. For example, the teacher may gain insight into ways to adapt the environment, adjust to a particular interaction style, or expand on a child's interest.

Infant care teachers use observation to learn children's interests, abilities, and needs. Teachers observe infants' and toddlers' ongoing behavior in familiar situations and settings without changing the environment, arranging special situations, or interacting with the children in scripted ways. Observation can be conducted in two ways. A team of two teachers may choose to have one teacher observe while the other goes about daily routines and interacts with the children. Another approach is to set up ways to record observations within daily routines, such as by taking notes, videotaping, or taking photos between or during events. Many teachers find different ways to combine these two approaches to fit the particular context in which the teachers work.

The teacher's observation notes can be used to complete the DRDP-R. In addition, the DRDP-R can serve as a guide for teachers as they attend to aspects of development while observing. The DRDP-R indicators and measures within indicators can help an infant care teacher focus on areas of development such as motor skills or self-regulation. For instance, a teacher may observe and record that when she brings out the clean diaper during a diaper change, a child stops moving and points at the diaper until the teacher says the word *diaper,* and then the child smiles and makes the sound *di.* This observation record could be used as the teacher determines whether the child is at the "Acting with Purpose" developmental level of the DRDP-R's "Communication and Language" indicator. As teachers gain experience in using the DRDP-R, they become more sensitive in observing behavior that indicates children's current level of learning and development.

While observing, the teacher routinely focuses on the child's interest. For instance, the teacher may see that a child watches, reaches for, and eventually approaches shiny things, such as a necklace, a metal bell, or the chrome water faucet. When the child picks up

Observing While Participating

One of the key challenges for infant care teachers is to be able to observe and record their observations while providing early care and education. Learning how to address this challenge takes time and a good support system. Teachers can develop plans together for observing and recording behavior in the context of daily routines and events. Some teachers take turns; others have systems such as cameras and note cards placed around the rooms and play yards so they can take quick notes or photos "on the fly." There are many ways to participate and observe at the same time. Children become accustomed to the teacher's taking notes and photos, and it becomes incorporated into the daily routines. Observations from teachers who are involved with children daily are really the most useful because the teacher understands the child's context; everything from how the child slept the night before to his current interests. Infant care teachers who observe regularly are better able to provide care and education that connects with each child in the group.

a shiny bell, it makes a noise, and she quickly learns to repeat the noise many times by shaking the bell. In exploring this object, she has made a discovery about cause-and-effect, which can be tested out on other objects. The teacher continually observes how the child explores such objects of interest and makes discoveries about them.

During observation the teacher may also notice and address barriers to learning. For example, the teacher may focus on whether the child can hear the soft ring of the bell when there are loud sounds nearby, such as the crying of a baby or tumbling block towers. An essential part of observation is identifying things that may take the child's attention away from exploration and discovery. Information about such barriers feeds directly into planning how to facilitate learning.

PROGRAMS:

- Hire staff members who have observation and recording skills or provide training to new and current staff members.
- Encourage teachers to observe as they participate in daily routines and events.

Preparation

- Set aside regularly scheduled time for child observation.
- Provide places for observation, such as an observation room or an adult chair away from the room's traffic flow.
- Provide the DRDP-R materials and training for infant care teachers.
- Supply observation tools (such as notepads, cameras).

"By observing and listening to children with care and attention, we can discover a way of truly seeing and getting to know them. By doing so we also become able to respect them for who they are and what they would like to communicate to us. We know that to an attentive eye and ear, infants communicate a great deal about themselves long before they can speak. Already at this stage, observing and listening is a reciprocal experience, because in observing how the children learn, we learn."

—L. Gandini and J. Goldhaber, in *Bambini: The Italian Approach to Infant/Toddler Care*

TEACHERS:

- Observe the behavior of the infants and toddlers throughout the entire day.

- Observe children when they are alone, with peers, with family members, and with caregivers.

- Watch carefully for infants' cues in order to respond to them appropriately.

- Observe children during times of spontaneous free activity.

- Incorporate observation and assessment processes in daily routines and activities.

Orientation

- Find some time to observe while not participating.

- Review the DRDP-R regularly and keep the indicators and themes in mind while observing behavior.

- Remain aware of the broad range of developmental differences in children even when they are of a similar age.

- Pay attention to children's activity levels, their biological rhythms, and their responses.

8.2

Teachers document observations for later use.

Recording observations allows teachers to gain additional insights about children's learning. Some teachers document observations by writing down what they see or by taking photographs. Other teachers record on videotape infants and toddlers exploring materials, trying out developing skills, and interacting with one another. Sometimes teachers use an observation form divided into categories, such as whether the child is alone or with other children. Teachers often create

forms that divide observation notes into areas of development: namely, motor development, social–emotional development, communication and language development, and cognitive development. Information from observation records is used to complete formal assessment profiles, such as the DRDP-R. To gain a complete picture of the developing child, teachers combine documentation strategies. Photos, observation notes, sketches, video-taped material, and assessment indicators can be used together to reflect on and understand the children's exploration and discovery.

PROGRAMS:

- Help teachers to develop an effective recordkeeping system that can be used by others.

- Obtain written permission from families to allow taking photographs, videotaping, and other forms of recording their children's learning.

- Adopt policies that protect children's confidentiality.

- Obtain documentation from other settings that also serve children enrolled in the program, when applicable and when

permission is granted in writing from the family.

Preparation

- Provide documentation tools.
- Provide time and space for documentation.
- Provide documentation training and guidance to teachers.

TEACHERS:

- Document each child's social–emotional, physical, cognitive, and language development based on teachers' observations and information from the family.
- Keep samples of older toddlers' drawings or paintings.

Tools

Use methods of recording observations that work for the whole team. For example:

- Take photographs.
- Make notes on note cards kept in pockets or in various places in the environment.
- Use an audiotape recorder.
- Use a video camera.
- Make sketches.

Recordkeeping

- Develop an effective recordkeeping system that can be used by others who have permission to gain access to such records.
- Maintain growth and development records, using checklists or forms that are consistent with the DRDP-R.

8.3

Teachers assess children's developmental progress.

Because the DRDP-R is based on observation, teachers can use their observation notes and other documentation to complete this assessment. They can then use information from the DRDP-R on individual children as a guide for planning. The DRDP-R identifies the developmental levels at which a child is operating. (See Table 3.) Understanding the child's developmental level in different domains helps teachers create ways to facilitate learning and development. For instance, using the DRDP-R, a teacher may have determined that a young infant is operating at the "Expanding Responses" developmental level on the DRDP-R measure of "Identity of Self and Connection to Others." She knows

---

Care for Children First While Observing and Documenting: Two Examples

Losing sight of the child's needs and setting up an artificial situation

Juan cries, and Maria thinks he's hungry. Maria goes to the food preparation area and begins to prepare his bottle. Juan calms down and watches her. Maria notices that Juan has calmed down and goes over to write it down on her observation notes. Juan watches Maria leave the kitchen area without a bottle. Juan begins to cry again. Maria realizes as she looks at her notes that she has never seen Juan grasp his own bottle. Maria finishes making Juan's bottle and places the bottle between his hands and uses only one of her fingers to hold up the bottle for feeding.

Meeting the child's needs and documenting naturally occurring behavior

Juan cries, and Maria recognizes his hunger cry. Maria moves close to Juan, looks in his eyes, puts her hand on him and says, "I think you are ready for a bottle. I will go get it for you." Maria goes to the food preparation area and begins to prepare his bottle. Juan calms down and watches her. She smiles at him and nods. Maria returns with the bottle and shows it to Juan. He reaches for her, she picks him up, and they settle together in a low chair. Juan touches the bottle and Maria's hand as Maria holds the bottle for him. After several minutes, Juan finishes the bottle, burps, and smiles sleepily at Maria. She loves that look on his face. Juan needs to stay upright for several minutes after his bottle so Maria carries him with her to the charts. She makes a note of how much he drank. She also notes that his hunger cry was recognizable to her, that he stopped crying when he saw she was getting a bottle (a sign that he can anticipate her actions and he trusts her), and that he touched the bottle for the first time today.

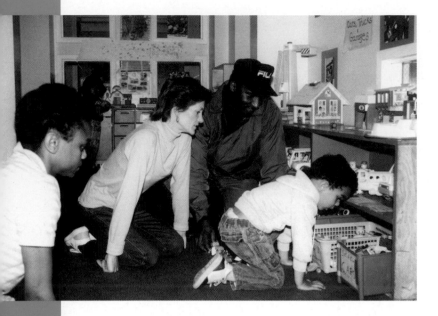

sets of developmental levels identify progress from left to right or from least advanced to most advanced.

PROGRAMS:

- Integrate the DRDP-R into the curriculum process.
- Provide assistance to teachers who are learning to record information in the DRDP-R and use it in the planning process.
- Provide teachers with planning time so that they can include assessments as part of the curriculum process.
- Communicate with families and staff members about the assessment of children's behavior, recognizing there is a wide range of typical behavior.

TEACHERS:

- Complete periodic assessments of each child using the DRDP-R.
- Track each child's developmental progress over time.
- Summarize DRDP-R assessment information on individual children in a form that can be easily used for curriculum planning.
- Include family members in the ongoing assessment process.

Recordkeeping

- Maintain a confidential file for each child with all DRDP-R assessment information.

that at this level, infants often learn by attending to other people's faces or voices for long periods of time. This information alerts the teacher to the child's interest in seeing and hearing other people. In the example, awareness of the child's developmental level helps the teacher be more sensitive to the child's potential interests.

Table 3 shows the two sets of levels that are used to identify developmental progress in a DRDP-R assessment of an infant or toddler. The first set of developmental levels is used to summarize a child's progress on each of the DRDP-R indicators; for example, "Self-Regulation" or "Cognitive Competence and Problem Solving Skills." The second set of developmental levels is used to summarize progress on the "Motor Skills" indicator. Both

Table 3. Levels of Developmental Progress in a DRDP-R Assessment of an Infant or Toddler

General DRDP-R Developmental Levels					
Responding with Reflexes	Expanding Responses	Acting with Purpose	Discovering Ideas	Developing Ideas	Connecting Ideas

Developmental Levels for Motor Skills					
Moving with Reflexes	Making Simple Movements	Coordinating Simple Movements	Exploring Complex Movements	Making Complex Movements	Expanding Complex Movements

Teachers take time to reflect on observations, documentation, and assessments.

Reflection is a way of looking back to look ahead. To make the most of observations, documentation, and assessments, teachers need time to think about or reflect on them. At first, reflection is open-ended and, if there is a team of teachers, may include one or more colleagues. The purpose is to understand what was observed and what resulted from formal assessments. During this first part of reflection, teachers use information given to them from the family, from their experience teaching, and from their knowledge of child development to interpret their observations and assessments of individual children. After arriving at an understanding of the observations and assessments, teachers consider how this new understanding might lead to the introduction of new materials or possibilities to explore for a child or small group of children. A teacher's perspective on the observation records and assessments is only one point of view. Teachers can expand their understanding of the observations and assessment information through discussions with family members and others who interact with the child regularly (such as specialists, health care providers, and others).

PROGRAMS:

- Provide time and space for reflection, which requires some physical and emotional distance from caregiving.
- Provide a format for reflection for those who need it, such as by dedicating a portion of staff meetings to open discussion.

TEACHERS:

- Slow down and take time to consider thoughts and feelings.
- Find a quiet place and set aside time to review documentation and assessment information.

Adapting Teaching and Caring Styles

Jack was a talkative and exuberant two-year-old. His mother brought him to Annalisa's family child care home each morning with his older sister Autumn, who was three. Jack would bound into the living room, greet the other children, and ask to play outside. He loved to play ball, chase, and climb. Annalisa always enjoyed Jack's enthusiasm for life and his resourcefulness when he played.

One morning Jack's mother, Jeri, told Annalisa that Jack had been diagnosed with asthma, and he had to take breathing treatments. Jeri was a nurse, and she helped Annalisa learn how to operate the nebulizer. Annalisa was surprised to observe that after Jack had his breathing treatment he seemed like a very different child. Little things that normally would not bother him made him cry loudly. One day he dropped a ball and cried and cried rather than pick it up. Annalisa was concerned and talked to Jeri about it. Jeri was concerned, too. She said she raised this issue with Jack's doctor, but he said the highest priority was clearly for Jack to breathe well. So Annalisa took some time over the weekend to look at her observation notes on Jack and to reflect on how she might handle this challenging situation.

On Sunday evening she called her friend Dorie, who was also a family child care provider, to talk about it. Talking with Dorie helped Annalisa see that she would need to adapt how she was interacting with Jack. Annalisa decided that she would start to get to know this new Jack, who emerged after the breathing treatments as if he had a different temperament. She felt she could adapt to that. She had known many other two-year olds who cried easily and needed extra help when things became difficult.

This new perspective helped her to anticipate Jack's needs. She stayed closer to him and offered assistance a bit sooner than previously. Seeing him struggle was difficult, but she was there for him when he needed her. Eventually, Jack was prescribed a different medication that did not affect him as intensely. This change was a relief for all involved, but Annalisa remembered for years to come how when Jack changed, she had to change, and this memory helped her in many other situations.

old materials may engage a child's curiosity and interest and speculate about the effects of novelty.

- Hypothesize, learn, guess, and adapt to the children and families.

- Discuss reflections with other teachers and a child's family members.

8.5

Teachers plan their approaches and the materials they will offer based on their observations, documentation, and reflections.

After teachers have reflected on their observation records and thought about ways to support or extend learning, they make plans to carry out these ideas and see what happens. These plans take into account general curriculum recommendations based on individual children's developmental levels as assessed by the DRDP.

- Consider how personal thoughts and feelings may have affected what has been observed and recorded.

Interpretation

- Speculate how different thoughts, feelings, and behaviors might relate to the behavior and responses of children and families.

- Use observations as a basis to think about how new materials or ways of presenting

PROGRAMS:

- Provide necessary play and learning materials.

- Provide time for staff members to plan and prepare the environment.

TEACHERS:

- Generate ideas, knowing that some will be used and others discarded.

- Consider the children's developmental levels that have been identified in the DRDPs.

- Examine all resulting ideas and select the most appropriate for implementation.

- Create brief, flexible written plans that are based on the responses and interests of the children.

Orientation

- Make plans that relate to what children actually do rather than to preconceived ideas about what children should or might do.

- Make decisions about how to support and extend a child's learning through interactions and changes to the environment.

8.6

Teachers implement their plans for facilitating learning.

The implementation process is closely linked with the first step of this process: observation. As a teacher tries out something new, such as placing baskets and balls of different sizes on the floor in the morning, she observes how the children respond to this change—and the cycle begins again. When implementing ideas, teachers must remember that children's responses may be surprising. Children may approach and interact with materials differently from how teachers imagined, or they may not approach the materials at all. Much can be learned through observation, documentation, and assessment but, during the infant/toddler years, each child is constantly changing and at any moment may present teachers with new interests, needs, or behavior. Part of what makes this work so invigorating is that, with very young children, teachers learn to expect the unexpected. As teachers implement their plans and eagerly await children's responses, they must remain flexible when ideas take a different turn. The curriculum process as presented in this publication is fluid enough so that infant care teachers can adapt to new interests and abilities as children continually change and grow.

PROGRAMS:

- Support teachers to implement plans in the spirit of experimentation; each time a plan works or does not work, teachers can learn and grow from the experience.

TEACHERS:

- Use the information gathered from the process of observing, documenting, assessing, reflecting, and planning to create a rich learning setting for each child and the group.

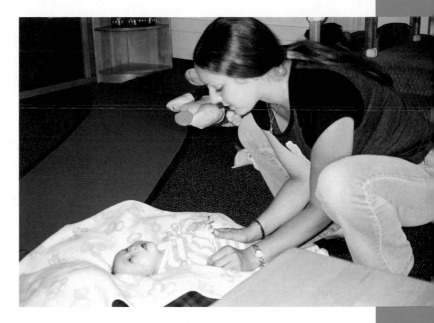

- Try out different ways to arrange materials, equipment, and areas in the environment to see how they work.
- Follow the children's lead as they interact with materials, the environment, and each other.
- Remain available to the child to answer questions (or even a questioning look) and offer assistance, when appropriate, for that particular child.

Orientation

- Trust the children to teach themselves as they interact with materials and other people in the environment.
- Interact with each child (such as by talking, listening, touching, watching, waiting, responding) to support the child's curiosity, exploration, and integration of new knowledge.

Part Three: Resources

Curriculum Resources

This section provides information on the videos, guides, and manuals created for the California Department of Education by the Program for Infant/Toddler Caregivers (PITC). These curriculum materials are being used throughout the state in the CDE's Partners for Quality program to provide training and technical assistance to local infant/toddler programs. They are also made available to practitioners at local resource and referral (R&R) programs. The CDE has provided each R&R with multiple copies of materials.

The Program for Infant/Toddler Caregivers: A Relationship-Based Curriculum

The PITC videos, guides, and manuals are designed to help program leaders and caregivers become sensitive to infants' cues, connect with their family and culture, and develop responsive, relationship-based care. The goal of PITC is to help caregivers recognize the crucial importance of giving tender, loving care and assistance in infants' intellectual development through an attentive reading of each child's cues. The training materials provide the foundation for a style of care in which caregivers study the infants in their care, reflect on and record information about the children's interests and skills, and search for ways to set the stage for the child's next learning encounters.

The PITC curriculum provides the framework for a series of comprehensive, broadcast quality videos exploring all facets of caring for infants and toddlers through their critical formative stages of development.

There are four easy-to-follow modules—Module I, Social–Emotional Growth and Socialization; Module II, Group Care; Module III, Learning and Development; and Module IV, Culture, Family, and Providers. Each module contains videos, video magazines, curriculum guides, and trainer's manuals providing strategies and structures that are based on sound developmental research and theory.

Module I: Social–Emotional Growth and Socialization

The video and video magazines for this module include:

- *First Moves: Welcoming a Child to a New Caregiving Setting*
- *Flexible, Fearful, or Feisty: The Different Temperaments of Infants and Toddlers*
- *Getting in Tune: Creating Nurturing Relationships with Infants and Toddlers*

The printed materials for this module include:

- *Infant/Toddler Caregiving: A Guide to Social–Emotional Growth and Socialization*
- *Module I Trainer's Manual*

Module II: Group Care

The video and video magazines for this module include:

- *It's Not Just Routine: Feeding, Diapering, and Napping Infants and Toddlers* (Second edition)
- *Respectfully Yours: Magda Gerber's Approach to Professional Infant/Toddler Care*
- *Space to Grow: Creating a Child Care Environment for Infants and Toddlers*
- *Together in Care: Meeting the Intimacy Needs of Infants and Toddlers in Groups*

The printed materials for this module include:

- *Infant/Toddler Caregiving: A Guide to Routines* (Second edition)

- *Infant/Toddler Caregiving: A Guide to Setting Up Environments*
- *Module II Trainer's Manual*

Module III: Learning and Development

The video and video magazines for this module include:

- *The Ages of Infancy: Caring for Young, Mobile, and Older Infants*
- *Discoveries of Infancy: Cognitive Development and Learning*
- *Early Messages: Facilitating Language Development and Communication*

The printed materials for this module include:

- *Infant/Toddler Caregiving: A Guide to Cognitive Development and Learning*
- *Infant/Toddler Caregiving: A Guide to Language Development and Communication*
- *Module III Trainer's Manual*

Module IV: Culture, Family, and Providers

The video and video magazines for this module include:

- *Essential Connections: Ten Keys to Culturally Sensitive Child Care*
- *Protective Urges: Working with the Feelings of Parents and Caregivers*

The printed materials for this module include:

- *Infant/Toddler Caregiving: A Guide to Creating Partnerships with Families*
- *Infant/Toddler Caregiving: A Guide to Culturally Sensitive Care*
- *Module IV Trainer's Manual*

Module V: Beginning Together: Caring for Infants and Toddlers with Disabilities and Other Special Needs in Inclusive Settings

- *Module V Trainer's Manual*

For ordering information, please see the California Department of Education Press Web site at http://www.cde.ca.gov/re/pn/rc/ or contact CDE Press at:

California Department of Education
  CDE Press, Sales Unit
  Sales Unit Business Hours:
  8 a.m. to 4:30 p.m., Monday through Friday
  1430 N Street, Suite 3207
  (Pacific Standard Time)
  Sacramento, CA 95814
  Telephone: (916) 445-1260
  sales@cde.ca.gov

Training Opportunities

This section provides information on the training offered by several programs and made available through the California Department of Education. These training opportunities are connected through the common PITC philosophy and curriculum. Programs can receive on-site training from certified trainers, or individuals can attend institutes to become a certified trainer.

The Program for Infant/Toddler Caregivers

The Program for Infant/Toddler Caregivers (PITC) Partners for Quality provides a subsidized training and technical assistance program for California's infant/toddler center, family child care, and license-exempt providers. Through the training, center-based staff and family child care providers explore the PITC philosophy, curriculum, and recommended practices. On-site support fits the needs of the program or individual family child care provider. PITC Partners for Quality is a collaboration of the Child Development Division of the California Department of Education and WestEd, Center for Child and Family Studies.

To learn more about training and technical assistance for your program, please contact WestEd, Center for Child and Family Studies, 180 Harbor Drive, Suite 112, Sausalito, CA 94965; telephone (415) 289-2300; Fax (415) 289-2301.

The California Program for Infant/Toddler Caregivers Trainer Institutes

The California Department of Education, Child Development Division, in conjunction with the WestEd Center for Child and Family Studies, conducts comprehensive PITC

Trainer Institutes for educators, program managers, and other professionals who are responsible for training caregivers.

These intensive Trainer Institutes help trainers to deepen their own understanding of the PITC philosophy and relationship-based curriculum and to acquire skills in the integrated presentation of the concepts contained in the PITC videos and guides. The institutes also support the efforts of caregivers and program managers to develop and implement policies that ensure high-quality standards of care. Activities include training sessions and other instructional exchanges with noted infant/toddler experts and core faculty from the California Department of Education and WestEd. Training sessions in each module also focus on adult learning and teaching strategies.

The California Institutes are open to all applicants regardless of state residency. Fellowships are available only for California residents. Applications for the California Trainer Institutes can be downloaded at the PITC Web site at http://www.pitc.org.

WestEd also conducts PITC Trainer Institutes outside California. These institutes are available nationally and internationally by arrangement. For information please contact WestEd, Center for Child and Family Studies, 180 Harbor Drive, Suite 112, Sausalito, CA 94965; telephone (415) 289-2300; Fax (415) 289-2301.

Beginning Together: Caring for Infants and Toddlers with Disabilities and Other Special Needs in Inclusive Settings

Beginning Together was created for the California Institute on Human Services, Sonoma State University, in collaboration with the California Department of Education, Child Development Division, and WestEd, Center for Child and Family Studies. Beginning Together is a project designed to help young children with disabilities or other special needs and their families to feel included in care and education programs.

The purpose of Beginning Together is to ensure that appropriate practices are promoted for children with special needs at early care and education programs. This purpose is accomplished through a "training of trainers" institute, regional outreach activities, revision/development of written materials, support to institute graduates, and support of inclusive practices in other PITC activities, such as the demonstration programs. For more information, please send an e-mail to office@beginningtogether.org or call (760) 471-3827.

Family Child Care at Its Best

Many working parents in California turn to family child care providers for a safe, nurturing environment. As information about child development expands, many providers seek opportunities to improve their knowledge, skills, and quality of care. The "Family Child Care at Its Best" series, offered through the Child Care Training Project of the Center for Human Services at UC Davis and funded by the California Department of Education, emphasizes the needs of children from birth to age three. The series aims to:

- Enhance the quality and safety of licensed family child care homes.

- Increase retention of existing family child care homes.

- Provide state and local agencies with data about training and technical assistance to meet the needs of licensed family child care homes.

- Expand links between family child care providers, R&R agencies, county welfare departments, and child care associations.

Each trainer has extensive experience in working with children and training adults. Currently, classes are offered in English and Spanish, with simultaneous translation available in other languages. Classes can also be taken for continuing education units or academic credit, and the courses are open to both licensed and license-exempt providers. For more information, please contact Diane Harkins, Program Director, (530) 757-8643, dharkins@unexmail.ucdavis.edu.

Organizations and Web Sites

The following agencies offer resources:

Child Care and Education

California Child Care Resource and Referral Network

111 New Montgomery Street
Seventh Floor
San Francisco, CA 94105
Telephone: (415) 882-0234
Fax: (415) 882-6233
E-mail: info@rrnetwork.org
Web site: http://www.rrnetwork.org

The California Child Care Resource and Referral Network was founded in 1980 as an association of resource and referral (R&R) agencies throughout the state. These R&Rs have grown into comprehensive agencies equipped to provide information, training, and support for parents, caregivers, other community-based agencies, employers, and government policymakers.

California Department of Education

CDE Press, Sales Unit
1430 N Street, Suite 3207
Sacramento, CA 95814-5901
Telephone: (800) 995-4099
Fax: (916) 323-0823
Web site: http://www.cde.ca.gov/re/pn/rc/

The *Educational Resources Catalog* from CDE Press contains information about publications, such as model curriculum standards; child development materials, which cover general curriculum, quality review, school-age care, special needs, and infant/toddler caregivers; and parent resources. The catalog may be ordered by telephone or through the Web site.

Child Care Bureau

U.S. Department of Health and Human Services
Administration for Children and Families
Switzer Building, Room 2046
370 L'Enfant Promenade, SW
Washington, DC 20447
Telephone: (202) 690-6782
Fax: (202) 690-5600
Web site: http://www.acf.hhs.gov/programs/ccb

The Child Care Bureau is dedicated to enhancing the quality, affordability, and availability of child care for all families. It operates the National Child Care Information Center as well as administering federal funds to states, territories, and tribes to assist low-income families gain access to quality child care. The site also has an extensive Frequently Asked Questions section and provides information on research, news, and government initiatives.

Child Care Law Center (CCLC)

221 Pine Street, Third Floor
San Francisco, CA 94104
Telephone: (415) 394-7144
Fax: (415) 394-7140
E-mail: info@childcarelaw.org
Web site: http://www.childcarelaw.org

The CCLC's primary objective is to use legal tools to foster the development of high-quality, affordable child care—for every child, every parent, and every community. The CCLC works to expand child care options, particularly for low-income families, and to ensure that children are safe and nurtured in care outside the home.

Family Child Care at Its Best

UC Davis Child Care Training Series
744 P Street, M.S. 19-48
Sacramento, CA 95814
Telephone: (916) 229-4500
Fax: (916) 229-4508
Web site: http://ccld.ca.gov/
FamilyChil_1789.htm

Family Child Care at Its Best is an organization that offers a series of workshops emphasizing the needs of children from birth to age three. The series aims to (1) enhance the quality and safety of licensed family child care homes; (2) increase retention of existing family child care homes; (3) provide state and local agencies with data about training and technical assistance to meet the needs of licensed family child care homes; and (4) expand links between family child care providers, resource and referral agencies, county welfare departments, and child care associations. See the Web site for information on class schedules and training locations.

National Association of Child Care Resource and Referral Agencies

NACCRRA
3101 Wilson Boulevard, Suite 350
Arlington, VA 22201
Telephone: (703) 341-4100
Fax: (703) 341-4101
Web site: http://www.naccrra.net

The NACCRRA is the national network of community-based child care R&R agencies. Families, child care providers, and communities share information about quality child care.

National Association for Family Child Care

5202 Pinemont Drive
Salt Lake City, UT 84123
Telephone: (801) 269-9338
Fax: (801) 268-9507
E-mail: nafcc@nafcc.org
Web site: http://www.nafcc.org

The National Association for Family Child Care (NAFCC) is a nonprofit organization dedicated to promoting quality child care by strengthening the profession of family child care. The goals of the association are to (1) strengthen state and local associations as the primary support system for individual family

child care providers; (2) promote a professional accreditation program that recognizes and encourages quality care for children; (3) represent family child care providers by acting as an advocate for their needs and collaborating with other organizations; (4) promote the diversity of the family child care profession through training, state, and local associations, public education, and board membership; and (5) deliver effective programs through strong organizational management.

National Association for the Education of Young Children (NAEYC)

1509 Sixteenth Street, NW
Washington, DC 20036-1426
Telephone: (800) 424-2460
Fax: (202) 328-1846
E-mail: naeyc@naeyc.org
Web site: http://www.naeyc.org

The NAEYC seeks to lead and consolidate the efforts of individuals and groups to achieve healthy development and constructive education for young children. It is devoted to ensuring the provision of high-quality early childhood programs. The *Early Childhood Resources Catalog* contains lists of materials covering all topics included in the *Infant/ Toddler Learning and Development Program Guidelines.* The catalog may be ordered by telephone or through the Web site. In addition to the online store, the site also offers information on professional development, public policy and awareness, and program accreditation.

National Child Care Information Center

10530 Rosehaven Street, Suite 400
Fairfax, VA 22030
Telephone: (800) 616-2242
Fax: (800) 716-2242
TTY: (800) 516-2242
E-mail: info@nccic.org
Web site: http://www.nccic.org

The National Child Care Information Center (NCCIC), a project of the Child Care Bureau, was established by the U.S. Department of Health and Human Services to complement, enhance, and promote child care information linkages to serve as a mechanism for supporting high-quality, comprehensive services for children and families. The center's activities also include publication of the *Child Care Bulletin*, state technical assistance, and national leadership forums.

National Institute of Child Health and Human Development (NICHD)

Study of Early Child Care (SECC)
P.O. Box 3006
Rockville, MD 20847
Telephone: (800) 370-2943
Fax: (301) 217-0792
TTY: (888) 320-6942
E-mail:
NICHDInformationResourceCenter@mail.nih.gov
Web site: http://www.nichd.nih.gov/od/secc/index.htm

The NICHD SECC is the most comprehensive child care study conducted to date to determine how variations in child care are related to children's development.

Program for Infant/Toddler Caregivers

180 Harbor Drive, Suite 112
Sausalito, CA 94965-1410
Telephone: (415) 289-2300
Fax: (415) 289-2301
Web site: http://www.pitc.org

This organization is a primary provider of caregiver training, videos, and online library resources developed collaboratively by the California Department of Education and WestEd for caregivers serving infants and toddlers.

Zero to Three

National Center for Infants, Toddlers, & Families
2000 M Street, NW, Suite 200
Washington, DC 20036
Telephone: (202) 638-1144
Web site: http://www.zerotothree.org

This established organization provides resources for both parents and professionals. Its aim is to promote the healthy development of infants and toddlers by supporting and strengthening families, communities, and those who work on their behalf. The site features parenting tips, brain development information, suggestions on how to make the most out of everyday moments with young

children, news about policy initiatives, training and consultation, professional networking and development, and a range of programs, services, publications, and reference guides, including multimedia resources for professionals available for purchase.

Bookstore Web Site: http://www.zerotothree.org/bookstore/
Bookstore Telephone: (800) 899-4301

Children with Disabilities or Other Special Needs

Beginning Together

Telephone: (760) 471-3827
Fax: (760) 471-3862
E-Mail: beginningtogether@cihs-south.org
Web site: http://www.sonoma.edu/cihs/BT/beginning.html

The purpose of Beginning Together is to ensure that children with special needs are incorporated and appropriate inclusive practices are promoted in the training and technical assistance provided by the existing cadre of CDE/WestEd-certified trainers in the PITC. Beginning Together was created for the California Institute on Human Services, Sonoma State University, in collaboration with the California Department of Education, Child Development Division, and WestEd, Center for Child and Family Studies as an inclusion support to the Program for Infant/Toddler Caregivers (PITC). This is accomplished through a "training of trainers" institute, regional outreach activities, revision/development of written materials, support to institute graduates, and support of inclusive practices in other PITC activities, such as the demonstration programs.

Civitas

1327 W. Washington Boulevard, Suite 3D
Chicago, IL 60607
Telephone: (312) 226-6700
Fax: (312) 226-6733
E-mail: contactus@civitas.org
Web site: http://www.civitas.org

The Civitas child trauma programs at Baylor College of Medicine address child maltreatment in several areas.

Council for Exceptional Children

CEC Publications
1110 North Glebe Road, Suite 300
Arlington, VA 22201-5704
Telephone: (888) 232-7733
Fax: (703) 264-9494
TTY: (703) 264-9446
E-mail: service@cec.sped.org
Web site: http://www.cec.sped.org

The CEC is an international professional organization dedicated to improving educational outcomes for individuals with exceptionalities, students with disabilities, and the gifted. It publishes journals, newsletters, and special education materials.

National Information Center for Children and Youth with Disabilities (NICHCY)

P.O. Box 1492
Washington, DC 20013
Telephone: (800) 695-0285
Fax: (202) 884-8441
E-mail: nichcy@aed.org
Web site: http://www.nichcy.org

The NICHCY is a national information center that provides information on disabilities and disability-related issues for families, administrators, and educators. The Web site, in both English and Spanish, offers publications, resources, and information about the Individuals with Disabilities Education Act (IDEA).

Office of Special Education Programs (OSEP)

Office of Special Education and Rehabilitative Services
U.S. Department of Education
400 Maryland Avenue, SW
Washington, DC 20202-7100
Telephone: (202) 245-7459
Web site: http://www.ed.gov/about/offices/list/osers/osep/index.html

OSEP is dedicated to improving results for infants, toddlers, children, and youths with disabilities (ages birth through twenty-one) by providing leadership and financial support to assist states and local districts. The Individuals with Disabilities Education Act authorizes formula grants to states and discretionary grants to institutions of higher education and other nonprofit organizations to support research, demonstrations, technical assistance and dissemination, technology and personnel development, and parent-training and information centers.

Programs for Infants and Toddlers with Disabilities

Children and Family Services Branch
California Department of Developmental Services
P.O. Box 944202
Sacramento, CA 94244-2020
Telephone: (916) 654-1690
TTY: (916) 654-2054
Web site: http://www.dds.ca.gov

This state site offers information related to government policies and developmental issues.

Policy

Children Now

1212 Broadway, 5th Floor
Oakland, CA 94612
Telephone: (510) 763-2444
Telephone: (800) CHILD-44
Fax: (510) 763-1974
E-mail: children@childrennow.org
Web site: http://www.childrennow.org

Children Now is a national organization that promotes community action and policy changes to improve children's quality of life, especially poor and at-risk children. Each year Children Now publishes a "report card" on family economics, health, education, and safety. Branches of this organization are located in the following cities:

Report Card 2004 and State of Our Children companion report are available at http://www.childrennow.org/california/index.html.

The Children's Defense Fund

25 E Street, NW
Washington, DC 20001
Telephone: (202) 628-8787
E-mail: cdfinfo@childrensdefense.org
Web site: http://www.childrensdefense.org

The mission of the Children's Defense Fund (CDF) is to leave no child behind and to ensure every child a Healthy Start, a Head

Start, a Fair Start, a Safe Start, and a Moral Start in life and successful passage to adulthood with the help of caring families and communities. The CDF is a strong advocate for children, paying particular attention to the needs of poor and minority children and those with disabilities.

Culture and Diversity

ASPIRA
1444 Eye Street, NW, Suite 800
Washington DC 20005
Telephone: (202) 835-3600
Fax: (202) 835-3613
E-mail: info@aspira.org
Web site: http://www.aspira.org

This organization aims to be an "investment in Latino youth" and offers a variety of programs and services for children. ASPIRA also offers programs for parents that focus on education and leadership development.

The Black Community Crusade for Children (BCCC)
The Children's Defense Fund
25 E Street, NW
Washington, DC 20001
Telephone: (202) 628-8787
Fax: (202) 662-3580
E-mail: cdfinfo@childrensdefense.org
Web site: http://www.childrensdefense.org/bccc/

Coordinated nationally by the Children's Defense Fund, the BCCC seeks to support the healthy development of Black children, tap into and strengthen Black communities, and assist and galvanize current Black leadership around specific goals for children. Its program activities include leadership training and development, intergenerational mentoring, interracial and interethnic communication, and interdisciplinary networking.

California Tomorrow
1904 Franklin Street, Suite 300
Oakland, CA 94612
Telephone: (510) 496-0220
Fax: (510) 496-0225

E-mail: ct411@californiatomorrow.org
Web site: http://www.californiatomorrow.org

A nonprofit organization, California Tomorrow conducts research, provides technical assistance to educators and others, and produces publications, all of which focus on building a fair and equitable multiracial and multicultural society.

The Child Care Diversity Project
Childcare Health Program
1581 LeRoy Avenue
Berkeley, CA 94708
Telephone: (510) 644-1000
Fax: (510) 525-4106
Web site: http://www.childcarehealth.org/currentActivities.php

The Childcare Health Program has updated the training curriculum for child care providers to increase awareness of biracial and bicultural issues. The curriculum is intended to support child care providers in integrating activities and materials on biracial and bicultural children into their existing training curricula.

The second edition of its publication *Serving Children in Biracial and Bicultural Families: A Diversity Curriculum for the Training of Child Care Providers* includes a video and posters to accompany the training manual.

Coalition for Asian American Children and Families
50 Broad Street, Suite 1701
New York, NY 10004
Telephone: (212) 809-4675
Fax: (212) 785-4601
Web site: http://www.cacf.org

This organization provides important statistics, resources, and a bulletin board for professionals and concerned individuals. The aim of the CACF Web site is to provide information about various Asian American communities, challenge the myth of the "model minority," offer culturally sensitive training, and advocate change for impoverished Asian American children.

Educational Equity Concepts

100 Fifth Avenue, Eighth Floor
New York, NY 10011
Telephone: (212) 243-1110
Fax: (212) 627-0407
E-mail: information@edequity.org
Web site: http://www.edequity.org

Serving both teachers and parents, this organization promotes bias-free learning through innovative programs and materials that are intended to decrease discrimination based on gender, race/ethnicity, disability, and level of family income. One resource of note is *Including All of Us: An Early Childhood Curriculum About Disability.*

Improving Access and Opportunity for Latinos in Early Childhood

55 Chapel Street
Newton, MA 02458-1060
Telephone: (617) 969-7100
Fax: (617) 244-3609
Web site: http://www.edc.org/CCF/latinos

This program seeks to strengthen programs by putting together research and practice, professional development, and influential policies.

National Association for Multicultural Education

733 15th Street, NW, Suite 430
Washington, DC 20005
Telephone: (202) 628-6263
Fax: (202) 628-6264
E-mail: name@nameorg.org
Web site: http://www.nameorg.org

This organization aims to achieve social, political, economic, and educational equity. The site offers information on publications, conferences, events, and a listserv or e-mail discussion group.

National Black Child Development Institute (NBCDI)

1101 15th Street, NW, Suite 900
Washington, DC 20005
Telephone: (202) 833-2220
Fax: (202) 833-8222
E-mail: moreinfo@nbcdi.org
Web site: http://www.nbcdi.org

The NBCDI works to improve and protect the quality of life of African American children. The institute provides and supports programs, workshops, and resources for children, their families, and communities in the areas of early health and education, child welfare, and parenting. In California local chapters are working on the community level in Los Angeles, Pasadena/Altadena, and Sacramento.

National Coalition of Education Activists (NCEA)

P.O. Box 15790
Philadelphia, PA 19103
Telephone: (215) 735-2418
E-mail: info@edactivists.org
Web site: http://www.nceaonline.org

The NCEA is a multiracial network and membership organization of parents, school staff, union and community activists, and children's advocates working for equitable and excellent public schools. The NCEA contributes to building a movement for excellent and equitable schools by:

- Helping activists develop their knowledge and skills

- Creating opportunities for multiracial groups of parents, educators, and community activists to discuss key education issues and their practical solution

- Linking individuals with activists and groups they can work with and learn from

- Providing wide-ranging, nontechnical referrals and information with an emphasis on action and a perspective that values equity (Resources for Better Schools)

- Developing and disseminating materials that translate information on key issues, policy, and research into nontechnical language (Action for Better Schools)

Native Child

P.O. Box 1797
Santa Fe, NM 87504
Telephone: (505) 820-2204
Fax: (800) 787-7001
E-mail: info@nativechild.com
Web site: http://www.nativechild.com

The main focus of Native Child is the development of bilingual curriculum materials for both native and nonnative classrooms. The Web site offers books and resources as well as a section on Head Start quality improvement, a German version of the site, and other important links.

Oyate

2702 Mathews Street
Berkeley, CA 94702
Telephone: (510) 848-6700
Fax: (510) 848-4815
E-mail: oyate@oyate.org
Web site: http://www.oyate.org

This organization offers resources, evaluation of texts and resource materials, teacher workshops on antibias issues, a catalog of multimedia resources, materials and posters, books for teachers, and recommended fiction.

Respecting Ethnic and Cultural Heritage (REACH)

307 N. Olympic Avenue, Suite 211
Arlington, WA 98223
Toll-free telephone: (800) 205-4932
Telephone: (360) 403-9631
Fax: (360) 403-9637
E-mail: reach@nwlink.com
Web site: http://www.reachctr.org

Providing cultural diversity services, the REACH Center assists with strategic planning and training for individuals and educational institutions through workshops and curriculum development.

Teaching Tolerance

c/o The Southern Poverty Law Center
400 Washington Avenue
Montgomery, AL 36104
Telephone: (334) 956-8200
Fax: (334) 956-8488
Web site: http://www.teachingtolerance.org

This comprehensive site for teachers, parents, and children promotes respect for differences and appreciation for diversity. Founded by the Southern Poverty Law Center, Teaching Tolerance serves as a clearinghouse of information about antibias programs, activities, and initiatives being implemented in schools across the country.

Wu Yee Children's Services

888 Clay Street, Lower Level
San Francisco, CA 94108
Telephone: (415) 391-4890
Fax: (415) 391-4976
E-mail: joylok@wuyee.org
Web site: http://www.wuyee.org

Wu Yee's Children's Services is a non-profit family and children's agency whose aim is to create a nurturing environment for children and their families by advocating on their behalf, empowering parents, and providing linguistically and culturally appropriate services. The agency also administers the SF CARES program, designed to promote the compensation and retention of committed and qualified teachers and providers to ensure quality services to children and families and to stimulate public awareness about the importance of quality child care. The Web site has a cohesive directory of community service links for Asian families and others.

Families

The Adolescent Family Life Program (AFLP)

Maternal and Child Health Branch
California Department of Health Services
1615 Capitol Avenue, MS 8306
Sacramento, CA 95814
Telephone: (916) 650-0285
Fax: (916) 650-0304
E-mail: MCHInet@dhs.ca.gov
Web site: http://www.mch.dhs.ca.gov/programs/aflp/

The Adolescent Family Life Program (AFLP), operated through the California Department of Health, works to ensure that adolescents, their families, and their social support systems will be served by effective, comprehensive networks of local programs and agencies. The AFLP provides many services to adolescent parents and their families, including facilitating access to health care resources, prenatal care, the development of educational and vocational goals, and pregnancy prevention.

AARP Grandparent Information Center
601 E Street, NW
Washington, DC 20049
Telephone: (888) 687-2277 (English and Spanish)
Fax: (202) 434-6474
E-mail: gic@aarp.org
Web site: http://www.aarp.org/families/grandparents/gic/a2004-01-16-grandparentsinfocenter.html

The AARP Grandparent Information Center provides online (1) tip sheets on a variety of topics (e.g., grandparents raising grandchildren, starting support groups, traveling with your grandchildren, and many more); (2) print publications in English and some in Spanish as well; (3) information on and referral to local support groups for grandparent caregivers through the national database and referral to legal services, including access to the AARP Legal Services Network benefits for AARP members; (4) referral to other organizations that have pertinent information for grandparents; (5) technical assistance and networking with local, state, and national organizations; (6) research about key legislation and public policy issues; (7) cosponsorship of local, state, and national grandparent events to share information and raise awareness about various grandparent issues; and (8) advocacy in collaboration with AARP's state affairs and legal advocacy groups.

Families and Work Institute
267 Fifth Avenue, Floor 2
New York, NY 10016
Telephone: (212) 465-2044
Fax: (212) 465-8637
Web site: http://www.familiesandwork.org/

Families and Work Institute (FWI) is a nonprofit center for research that provides data for informed decision making on the changing workforce, family, and community. Founded in 1989, the institute offers some of the most comprehensive research on the U.S. workforce available. In 2003, the institute released *Highlights of the National Study of the Changing Workforce*, the 2002 edition of the largest and most far-reaching study of a representative sample of U.S. workers. This publication and others are available on the Web site.

Family Support America
205 West Randolph Street, Suite 2222
Chicago, IL 60606
Telephone: (312) 338-0900
Fax: (312) 338-1522
Web site: http://www.familysupportamerica.org

Formerly known as Family Resource Coalition of America, Family Support America promotes family support by identifying and connecting individuals and organizations that have contact with families; providing technical assistance, training and education, conferences, and publications; and promoting the voice of families. The organization offers information on parenting and on starting parent support groups.

The Center on Fathers, Families, and Public Policy
23 N. Pinckney Street, Suite 210
Madison, WI 53703
Telephone: (608) 257-3148
Fax: (608) 257-4686
Web site: http://www.cffpp.org

This nationally focused organization conducts policy research. It also provides technical assistance, training, and education to the public to focus on the barriers faced by never-married, low-income fathers and their families.

Teachers and Program Leaders

Building Child Care (BCC)
National Economic Development and Law Center
2201 Broadway, Suite 815
Oakland, CA 94612
Telephone: (888) 411-3535
E-mail: bcc@nedlc.org
Web site: http://www.buildingchildcare.org

The BCC Project, funded by the California Department of Education, is a collaboration of organizations designed to help child care providers gain access to public and private sector financing for child care facilities. The four collaborative partners on this project have combined their experience, resources, and expertise to build a clearinghouse of information and assistance for developing and financing child care facilities. The site also provides related links to other Web sites.

Center for the Child Care Workforce (CCW)

555 New Jersey Avenue, NW
Washington, DC 20001
Telephone: (202) 662-8005
Fax: (202) 662-8006
E-mail: ccw@aft.org
Web site: http://www.ccw.org

The CCW, a partner with the American Federation of Teachers Educational Foundation (AFTEF), sponsors Worthy Wage Day and coordinated the Worthy Wage movement. This organization's mission is to improve the quality of early care and education for all children by promoting policy that ensures the early care and education workforce is well educated, receives better compensation, and has a voice in the workplace. The Web site includes many informative publications free of charge that teachers, directors, and policymakers can order.

Resources for Infant Educarers (RIE)

1550 Murray Circle
Los Angeles, CA 90026
Telephone: (323) 663-5330
Fax: (323) 663-5586
E-mail: educarer@rie.org
Web site: http://www.rie.org

The RIE is a nonprofit organization that has developed a unique methodology in working with infants called "Educaring," based on respect. The Web site offers information on professional certification training, parent-infant classes, excerpts from the writings of its founding director Magda Gerber, and online ordering of audio- and videotapes, books, and other resources for parents and professionals.

Teen Parents

California Alliance Concerned with School-Age Parenting and Pregnancy Prevention

CACSAP
8367 Lemon Avenue
La Mesa, CA 91941
Telephone: (619) 741-6756
E-mail: cacsap@hotmail.com
Web site: http://www.cacsap.org

The CACSAP is dedicated to promoting the health and well-being of expectant and parenting teenagers and their young children and preventing adolescent childbearing. Established in 1971, the CACSAP represents educators, social workers, health care providers, parents, policymakers, and others committed to supporting both teenagers who experience early pregnancy and childbearing and children of young parents. The CACSAP is also committed to preventing early sexual activity or repeat pregnancy among adolescents.

Healthy Teen Network, Inc.

509 Second Street, NE
Washington, DC 20002
Telephone: (202) 547-8814
Fax: (202) 547-8815
E-mail:
HealthyTeens@HealthyTeenNetwork.org
Web site: http://
www.healthyteennetwork.org

This organization's mission is to provide general leadership, education, training, information, advocacy, resources, and support to individuals and organizations in the field of adolescent pregnancy, parenting, and pregnancy prevention. The Web site includes resources (including an electronic clearinghouse), relevant publications, and information on conferences of the National Organization on Adolescent Pregnancy, Parenting, and Prevention.

Parents and the Law Program

Street Law, Inc.
1010 Wayne Avenue, Suite 870
Silver Spring, MD 20910
Telephone: (301) 589-1130
Fax: (301) 589-1131
E-mail: clearinghouse@streetlaw.org
Web site: http://www.streetlaw.org/tpal.html

Street Law administers the Parents and the Law Program: Teaching Young Parents Practical Law and Life Skills. Teen parents need to know how the law can protect their families and promote their self-sufficiency. Street Law affirms that teaching teen parents the law, through educational strategies that enhance their life skills and community bonds, is an important part of the response to the multifaceted problem of teenage parents. This site can aid infant/toddler caregivers who work with teenage parents of all backgrounds who face custody concerns, child support issues, and other legal matters.

Cal-Learn Program

Web site: http://www.dss.cahwnet.gov/ cdssweb/Cal-Learn_170.htm#PageTop

As a strategy for reducing teen pregnancy rates and long-term welfare dependency, the Cal-Learn Program was designed to assist teen parents receiving assistance through the California Work Opportunity and Responsibility to Kids (CalWORKs) program. The Cal-Learn program, operated by the California Department of Social Services, helps pregnant and parenting teens to attend and graduate from high school or its equivalent. This ambitious effort consists of three coordinated services designed to help teens become self-sufficient adults and responsible parents: (1) intensive case management assists teen parents to obtain education, health, and social services; (2) payments for necessary child care, transportation, and educational expenses enable pregnant and parenting teens to attend school; and (3) bonuses and sanctions encourage school attendance and good grades.

Health and Safety

California Childcare Health Program

1333 Broadway, Suite 1010
Oakland, CA 94612-1926
Telephone: (800) 333-3212 (Healthline)
Fax: (510) 839-0339
Web site: http:// www.ucsfchildcarehealth.org/html/ healthline/healthlinemain.htm

Healthline is a project created for the use of all child care center staff, family child care providers, and parents who use child care in California. Administered by the California Childcare Health Program, Healthline is staffed by bilingual public health nurses experienced in child care and infant health. The toll-free telephone number provides consultation on concerns dealing with special needs, behavioral health, nutrition, car seat safety, and infant and toddler behavior. Workshops and technical assistance for child care providers and agencies are other services provided by the California Child Care Healthline.

Healthy Families America (HFA)

200 S. Michigan Avenue, Suite 1700
Chicago, IL 60604
Telephone: (312) 663-3520
Fax: (312) 939-8962
Web site: http:// www.healthyfamiliesamerica.org

The HFA strives to provide all expectant and new parents with the opportunity to receive the education and support they need at the time their baby is born. The organization offers information for a healthy start and provides services to overburdened families.

Medline Plus

Web site: http://www.nlm.nih.gov/ medlineplus

The U.S. National Library of Medicine and the National Institutes of Health offer a comprehensive Web site. It features an alphabetical online list of articles on various health topics such as infant and toddler health, infant and newborn care, and infant and toddler development.

National Resource Center for Health and Safety in Child Care

UCHSC at Fitzsimons
Campus Mail Stop F541; P.O. Box 6508
Aurora, CO 80045-0508
Telephone: (800) 598-KIDS (-5437)
Fax: (303) 724-0960
E-mail: natl.child.res.ctr@uchsc.edu
Web site: http://nrc.uchsc.edu

This site provides information on evaluating child care settings and state licensure regulations, including topics such as ill children in child care facilities, SIDS risk reduction, and performance standards reports.

ChildHelp USA, National Crisis Hotline
15757 N. 78th Street
Scottsdale, AZ 85260
Telephone: (480) 922-8212
Toll-free: (800) 4-A-CHILD
Fax: (480) 922-7061
E-mail: help@childhelpusa.org
Web site: http://childhelpusa.org

A 24-hour, toll-free, confidential hotline offers information about the treatment and prevention of child abuse. ChildHelp USA provides crisis counseling to adult survivors and child victims of child abuse, offenders, and parents.

Infant Mental Health

Center on the Social and Emotional Foundations for Early Learning
University of Illinois at Urbana-Champaign
Children's Research Center
51 Gerty Drive
Champaign, IL 61820
Telephone: (217) 333-4123 or (877) 275-3227
Fax: (217) 244-7732
E-mail: csefel@uiuc.edu
Web site: http://csefel.uiuc.edu

As part of the U.S. Department of Health and Human Services Administration for Children and Families, the center focuses on strengthening the capacity of child care and Head Start programs to improve the social and emotional outcomes of young children.

Federation of Families for Children's Mental Health (FFCMH)
1101 King Street, Suite 420
Alexandria, VA 22314
Telephone: (703) 684-7710
Fax: (703) 836-1040
E-mail: ffcmh@ffcmh.org
Web site: http://www.ffcmh.org

The FFCMH is a national parent-run nonprofit organization focused on the needs of children and youths with emotional, behavioral, or mental disorders and their families.

Mental Health Association in California
1127 11ᵗʰ Street, Suite 925
Sacramento, CA 95814
Telephone: (916) 557-1167
E-mail: swelch@mhac.org
Web site: http://www.mhac.org

The mission of the MHAC is to provide advocacy, education, information, and other assistance necessary to ensure that all people who require mental health services are able to receive them and are not denied any other benefits, services, rights, or opportunities due to their need for mental health services. This site has links and contact information for immediate help.

National Mental Health Association
2001 N. Beauregard Street, 12th Floor
Alexandria, VA 22311
Telephone: (703) 684-7722
Toll-free: (800) 969-NMHA (6642)
TTY: (800) 433-5959
Fax: (703) 684-5968
Web site: http://www.nmha.org

With more than 340 nationwide affiliates, the NMHA is the country's oldest and largest nonprofit organization addressing all aspects of mental health and mental illness. The Web site features the latest news on national public policy regarding mental health issues, as well as sections on advocacy, research, education, and service. The NMHA has a bookstore and general mental health information.

World Association for Infant Mental Health
University Outreach & Engagement
Kellogg Center, Garden Level, #24
Michigan State University
East Lansing, MI 48824
Telephone: (517) 432-3793
Fax: (517) 432-3694
E-mail: waimh@msu.edu
Listserve: listserve@list.msu.edu
Web site: http://www.msu.edu/user/waimh

The WAIMH is an international and interdisciplinary organization concerned with the optimal development of infants and caregiver-infant relationships. It promotes education, research, and study of the effects of mental development during infancy on later normal and psychopathological development; research and study of the mental health of the parents, families, and other caregivers of infants; and the development of scientifically based programs of care, intervention, and prevention of mental impairment in infancy. The WAIMH also sponsors regional and world congresses devoted to scientific, educational, and clinical work with infants and their caregivers. It provides quarterly newsletters, computer-based information technology, and the development of affiliate associations around the world. The *Infant Mental Health Journal* is its official publication.

Zero to Three, Infant Mental Health Resource Center

Zero to Three
National Center for Infants, Toddlers, and Families
2000 M Street, NW, Suite 200
Washington, DC 20036
Telephone: (202) 638-1144
Web site: http://www.zerotothree.org/imh

This site offers resources and information regarding infant mental health and social–emotional health.

ERIC Resources

Last year, the U.S. Department of Education closed the 16 federally financed ERIC clearinghouses as part of its effort to revamp and centralize the Educational Resources Information Center (ERIC). Although a single new contractor prepares its online system, many materials archived in the former system remain available.

The central online database can be found at http://www.eric.ed.gov. In addition, many former clearinghouses have established new locations for their files, and users may find it less expensive to obtain materials through these Web sites. The topics are listed here in alphabetical order.

- Adult, Career, and Vocational Education: http://www.cete.org/acve
- Assessment and Evaluation: http://edresearch.org
- Counseling and Student Services: http://counselingoutfitters.com
- Disabilities and Gifted Education: http://www.cec.sped.org
- Educational Management: http://cepm.uoregon.edu
- Elementary and Early Childhood Education: http://ecap.crc.uiuc.edu/info
- Information and Technology: http://www.eduref.org
- Languages and Linguistics: http://www.cal.org
- Reading, English, and Communication: http://www.kidscanlearn.com
- Rural Education and Small Schools: http://www.edvantia.org
- Science, Mathematics, and Environmental Education: http://stemworks.org
- Social Studies/Social Science Education: http://www.indiana.edu/~ssdc/ssdc.htm
- Teaching and Teacher Education: http://www.aacte.org
- Urban Education: http://iume.tc.columbia.edu

The Educators Reference Desk (www.eduref.org) provides the familiar search interface to the ERIC database and some resources that were created by AskERIC before it closed.

Appendixes

Appendix A

Summary of Infant/Toddler Learning and Development Guidelines

Guidelines for Operating Infant/Toddler Programs

Section 1: Providing FAMILY-Oriented Programs

1.1 Programs and teachers support the relationship between the family and the child as the primary relationship in a child's life.

1.2 Programs and teachers are responsive to cultural and linguistic diversity.

1.3 Programs and teachers build relationships with families.

Section 2: Providing RELATIONSHIP-Based Care

2.1 Programs and teachers provide intimate, relationship-based care for infants and toddlers.

2.2 Programs and teachers ensure that all children have a sense of belonging.

2.3 Programs and teachers personalize care routines for infants and toddlers.

Section 3: Ensuring HEALTH and SAFETY

3.1 Programs and teachers promote the physical health of all children.

3.2 Programs and teachers ensure the safety of all children.

3.3 Programs and teachers ensure that children are well nourished and enjoy mealtimes.

3.4 Programs and teachers promote children's mental health.

3.5 Programs and teachers protect all children from abuse and neglect.

Section 4: Creating and Maintaining ENVIRONMENTS for Infants and Toddlers

4.1 Both indoor and outdoor spaces support the development of a small community of families, teachers, and infants, where relationships of care and trust are built.

4.2 The environment is safe and comfortable for all children, teachers, and family members.

4.3 The environment is arranged and organized to support children's free movement.

4.4 The environment is organized and prepared to support children's learning interests and focused exploration.

Section 5: Engaging in PROGRAM Development and Commitment to Continuous Improvement

5.1 Programs meet quality standards.

5.2 Programs monitor the development of individual infants and toddlers.

5.3 Programs engage in systematic self-assessment.

5.4 Programs develop and maintain partnerships within their community.

Section 6: Helping TEACHERS Continue to Grow Professionally

6.1 Programs hire well-qualified, representative staff members.

6.2 Programs create working conditions that support quality and job satisfaction to reduce turnover.

6.3 Programs foster respectful, collaborative relationships among adults.

6.4 Programs support the professional development and ethical conduct of infant care teachers and program leaders.

6.5 Programs use reflective supervision to support teachers.

Guidelines for Facilitating Learning and Development with Infants and Toddlers

Section 7: Understanding that LEARNING AND DEVELOPMENT Are Integrated Across Domains (Physical, Social–Emotional, Language and Communication, and Cognitive)

7.1 Teachers pursue professional development opportunities to better support the learning and development of infants and toddlers.

7.2 Programs and teachers facilitate learning across domains.

7.3 Programs and teachers facilitate physical development and learning.

7.4 Programs and teachers facilitate social–emotional development and learning.

7.5 Programs and teachers provide guidance for social behavior.

7.6 Programs and teachers facilitate language and communication development and learning.

7.7 Programs and teachers nurture a love of books and stories.

7.8 Programs and teachers facilitate cognitive development.

Section 8: Implementing an Infant/Toddler CURRICULUM Process

8.1 Teachers observe children during personal care routines, interactions, and play.

8.2 Teachers document observations for later use.

8.3 Teachers assess children's developmental progress.

8.4 Teachers take time to reflect on their observations, documentation, and assessments.

8.5 Teachers plan their approaches and the materials they will offer based on their observations, documentation, and reflections.

8.6 Teachers implement their plans for facilitating learning.

Appendix B

California's Early Start Program

Part C of the Individuals with Disabilities Education Act (IDEA) is the federal law that addresses services for infants and toddlers, and the California Early Intervention Services Act is the state law that implements the IDEA. California's Early Start program is the state's early intervention program for infants and toddlers from birth through 36 months of age and is guided by both federal and state law. The Department of Developmental Services is the lead agency for Early Start and collaborates with the Department of Education, Department of Social Services, and several other state agencies to provide services to infants and toddlers who have a developmental disability or who are at risk of developmental disabilities. Children and families eligible for the Early Start Program qualify for early intervention services. Regional centers share primary responsibility with local educational agencies (LEAs), such as school districts and county offices of education, for coordinating and providing early intervention services at the local level. Services may include specialized instruction, speech and language services, physical and/or occupational therapy, and transportation.

Infants and toddlers may be identified and referred to regional centers or LEAs through primary referral sources in their communities, including hospitals, health care providers, child care providers, LEAs, social service programs, or the child's family. Each infant or toddler referred to Early Start receives an evaluation to determine eligibility and an assessment to determine service needs if eligible. The individualized family services plan (IFSP) is the legal document that describes the services the child is receiving.

IFSPs are reviewed at least every six months and early care and education (ECE) providers are welcome to participate in these meetings with the permission of parents. The participation of ECE providers in these meetings could be especially important if the child is receiving any early intervention services on-site in the ECE setting.

Federal and state laws emphasize that early intervention services should be provided in "natural environments" whenever possible. Natural environments are those places where the child and family would be, such as the home or a child care program, if the child did not have a disability. Therefore, a parent may approach service providers about providing intervention services on-site in the child care program. Welcoming a therapist or an early interventionist into ECE settings is a positive way to promote inclusion and enriches the program as a whole.

Early Start also provides funding for 55 family resource centers to provide parent-to-parent support to families of infants and toddlers with special needs. These Family Resource Centers/Networks (FRCNs) are staffed primarily by parents and provide support in a nonclinical, family-centered environment. FRCNs provide referral information and outreach to underserved populations, support child-find activities and family/professional collaborative activities, and assist families with transition.

Source: L. M. Brault, J. P. Knapp, and P. J. Winton, "School Readiness for ALL Children: Ensuring That Children with Disabilities or Other Special Needs Are Included in California's School Readiness Efforts," in *First 5 School Readiness Initiative Technical Assistance Project.* Los Angeles: UCLA Center for Healthier Children, Families, and Communities, 2003.

Appendix C

Linking the Infant/Toddler Learning and Development Guidelines to the DRDP-R

Desired Result	Theme	Indicator	7.2 Programs and teachers facilitate learning across domains.	7.3 Programs and teachers facilitate physical development and learning.	7.4 Programs and teachers facilitate social-emotional development and learning.	7.5 Programs and teachers provide guidance for social behavior.	7.6 Programs and teachers facilitate language and communication development and learning.	7.7 Programs and teachers nurture a love of books and stories.	7.8 Programs and teachers facilitate cognitive development.	2.3 Programs and teachers personalize care routines for infants and toddlers.	3.2 Programs and teachers ensure the safety of all children.
Desired Result 1: Children are personally and socially competent	Self awareness and a positive self concept	1: Identity of self and connection to others	✓		✓						
		2: Recognition of ability	✓		✓						
		3: Self expression	✓		✓						
		4: Awareness of diversity	✓		✓						
	Social and interpersonal skills	5: Empathy	✓		✓	✓					
		6: Interaction with adults	✓		✓						
		7: Relationships with familiar adults	✓		✓						
		8: Relationships with familiar peers	✓		✓	✓					
		9: Interactions with peers	✓		✓	✓					
	Self regulation	10: Impulse control	✓		✓	✓					
		11: seeking others help to regulate self	✓		✓	✓					
		12: Responsive to others support	✓		✓	✓					
		13: Self comforting	✓		✓	✓					
	Communication and language	14: Attention maintenance	✓		✓	✓					
		15: Language comprehension	✓				✓	✓			
		16: Responsiveness to language	✓				✓	✓			
		17: Communication of needs, feelings, and interests	✓				✓				
		18: Reciprocal communication	✓				✓	✓			
Desired Result 2: Children are effective learners	Cognitive competence problem solving	19: Memory	✓						✓		
		20: Cause and effect	✓						✓		
		21: Problem solving	✓						✓		
		22: Symbolic play	✓						✓		
		23: Curiosity	✓						✓		
	Mathematical concepts	24: Number	✓						✓		
		25: Space and size	✓						✓		
		26: Time	✓						✓		
		27: Classification and matching	✓						✓		
	Literacy[1]	28: Interest in literacy	✓					✓			
		29: Recognition of symbols	✓					✓			
DR 3: Physical and motor competence	Motor skills	30: Gross motor	✓	✓							
		31: Fine motor	✓	✓							
		32: Balance	✓	✓							
		33: Eye-hand coordination	✓	✓							
DR 4: Safe and healthy	Safe and healthy	34: Personal care routines	✓							✓	
		35: Safety	✓								✓

Appendix D

NAEYC Code of Ethical Conduct and Statement of Commitment

A position statement of the National Association for the Education of Young Children

Revised April 2005

Preamble

NAEYC recognizes that those who work with young children face many daily decisions that have moral and ethical implications. The NAEYC Code of Ethical Conduct offers guidelines for responsible behavior and sets forth a common basis for resolving the principal ethical dilemmas encountered in early childhood care and education. The Statement of Commitment is not part of the Code but is a personal acknowledgment of an individual's willingness to embrace the distinctive values and moral obligations of the field of early childhood care and education.

The primary focus of the Code is on daily practice with children and their families in programs for children from birth through 8 years of age, such as infant/toddler programs, preschool and prekindergarten programs, child care centers, hospital and child life settings, family child care homes, kindergartens, and primary classrooms. When the issues involve young children, then these provisions also apply to specialists who do not work directly with children, including program administrators, parent educators, early childhood adult educators, and officials with responsibility for program monitoring and licensing. (Note: See also the Code of Ethical Conduct: "Supplement for Early Childhood Adult Educators," online at http://www.naeyc.org/about/positions/pdf/ethics04.pdf.)

Core Values

Standards of ethical behavior in early childhood care and education are based on commitment to core values that are deeply rooted in the history of the field of early childhood care and education. We have made a commitment to

- Appreciate childhood as a unique and valuable stage of the human life cycle
- Base our work with children on knowledge of how children develop and learn
- Appreciate and support the bond between the child and family
- Recognize that children are best understood and supported in the context of family, culture,[1] community, and society
- Respect the dignity, worth, and uniqueness of each individual (child, family member, and colleague)
- Respect diversity in children, families, and collegues
- Recognize that children and adults achieve their full potential in the context of relationships that are based on trust and respect

Conceptual Framework

The Code sets forth a framework of professional responsibilities in four sections. Each section addresses an area of professional relationships: (1) with children, (2) with families, (3) among colleagues, and (4) with the community and society. Each section includes an introduction to the primary responsibilities of the early childhood practitioner in that context. The introduction is followed by a set of ideals (I) that reflect exemplary professional practice and by a set of principles (P) describing practices that are required, prohibited, or permitted.

The ideals reflect the aspirations of practitioners. The principles guide conduct and assist practitioners in resolving ethical dilemmas.[2] Both ideals and principles are intended to direct practitioners to those questions which, when responsibly answered, can provide the basis for conscientious decision making. While the Code provides specific direction for addressing some ethical dilemmas, many others will require the practitioner to combine the guidance of the Code with professional judgment.

---

[1]The term *culture* includes ethnicity, racial identity, economic level, family structure, language, and religious and political beliefs, which profoundly influence each child's development and relationship to the world.

[2]There is not necessarily a corresponding principle for each ideal.

The ideals and principles in this Code present a shared framework of professional responsibility that affirms our commitment to the core values of our field. The Code publicly acknowledges the responsibilities that we in the field have assumed, and in so doing supports ethical behavior in our work. Practitioners who face ethical dimensions are urged to seek guidance in the applicable parts of this Code and in the spirit that informs the whole.

Often "the right answer"—the best ethical course of action to take—is not obvious. There may be no readily apparent, positive way to handle a situation. When one important value contradicts another, we face an ethical dilemma. When we face a dilemma, it is our professional responsibility to consult the Code and all relevant parties to find the most ethical resolution.

Section I: Ethical Responsibilities to Children

Childhood is a unique and valuable stage in the human life cycle. Our paramount responsibility is to provide care and education in settings that are safe, healthy, nurturing, and responsive for each child. We are committed to supporting children's development and learning; respecting individual differences; and helping children learn to live, play, and work cooperatively.

Ideals

I-1.1. To be familiar with the knowledge base of early childhood care and education and to stay informed through continuing education and training.

I-1.2. To base program practices upon current knowledge and research in the field of early childhood education, child development, and related disciplines, as well as on particular knowledge of each child.

I-1.3. To recognize and respect the unique qualities, abilities, and potential of each child.

I-1.4. To appreciate the vulnerability of children and their dependence on adults.

I-1.5. To create and maintain safe and healthy settings that foster children's social, emotional, cognitive, and physical development and that respect their dignity and their contributions.

I-1.6. To use assessment instruments and strategies that are appropriate for the children to be assessed, that are used only for the purposes for which they were designed, and that have the potential to benefit children.

I-1.7. To use assessment information to understand and support children's development and learning, to support instruction, and to identify children who may need additional services.

I-1.8. To support the right of each child to play and learn in an inclusive environment that meets the needs of children with and without disabilities.

I-1.9. To advocate for and ensure that all children, including those with special needs, have access to the support services needed to be successful.

I-1.10. To ensure that each child's culture, language, ethnicity, and family structure are recognized and valued in the program.

I-1.11. To provide all children with experiences in a language that they know, as well as support children in maintaining the use of their home language and in learning English.

I-1.12. To work with families to provide a safe and smooth transition as children and families move from one program to the next.

Principles

P-1.1. Above all, we shall not harm children. We shall not participate in practices that are emotionally damaging, or physically harmful disrespectful, degrading, dangerous, exploitative, or intimidating to children. *This principle has precedence over all others in this Code.*

P-1.2. We shall care for and educate children in positive emotional and social environments that are cognitively stimulating and that support each child's culture, language, ethnicity, and family structure.

P-1.3. We shall not participate in practices that discriminate against children by denying benefits, giving special advantages, or excluding them from programs or activities on the basis of their sex, race, national origin, religious beliefs, medical condition, disability, or the marital status/family structure, sexual orientation, or religious beliefs or other affiliations of their families. (Aspects of this principle do not apply in programs that have a lawful mandate to provide services to a particular population of children.)

P-1.4. We shall involve all those with relevant knowledge (including families and staff) in decisions concerning a child, as appropriate, ensuring confidentiality of sensitive information.

P-1.5. We shall use appropriate assessment systems, which include multiple sources of information, to provide information on children's learning and development.

P-1.6. We shall strive to ensure that decisions such as those related to enrollment, retention, or assignment to special education services, will be based on multiple sources of information and will never be based on a single assessment, such as a test score or a single observation.

P-1.7. We shall strive to build individual relationships with each child; make individualized adaptations in teaching strategies, learning environments, and curricula; and consult with the family so that each child benefits from the program. If after such efforts have been exhausted, the current placement does not meet a child's needs, or the child is seriously jeopardizing the ability of other children to benefit from the program, we shall collaborate with the child's family and appropriate specialists to determine the additional services needed and/or the placement options(s) most likely to ensure the child's success. (Aspects of this principle may not apply in programs that have a lawful mandate to provide services to a particular population of children.)

P-1.8. We shall be familiar with the risk factors for and symptoms of child abuse and neglect, including physical, sexual, verbal, and emotional abuse and physical, emotional, educational, and medical neglect. We shall know and follow state laws and community procedures that protect children against abuse and neglect.

P-1.9. When we have reasonable cause to suspect child abuse or neglect, we shall report it to the appropriate community agency and follow up to ensure that appropriate action has been taken. When appropriate, parents or guardians will be informed that the referral has been made.

P-1.10. When another person tells us of his or her suspicion that a child is being abused or neglected, we shall assist that person in taking appropriate action in order to protect the child.

P-1.11. When we become aware of a practice or situation that endangers the health, safety, or well-being of children, we have an ethical responsibility to protect children or inform parents and/or others who can.

Section II: Ethical Responsibilities to Families

Families[3] are of primary importance in children's development. Because the family and the early childhood practitioner have a common interest in the child's well-being, we acknowledge a primary responsibility to bring about communication, cooperation, and collaboration between the home and early childhood program in ways that enhance the child's development.

---

[3]The term *family* may include those adults, besides parents, with the responsibly of being involved in educating, nurturing, and advocating for the child.

Ideals

I-2.1. To be familiar with the knowledge base related to working effectively with families and to stay informed through continuing education and training.

I-2.2. To develop relationships of mutual trust and create partnerships with the families we serve.

I-2.3. To welcome all family members and encourage them to participate in the program.

I-2.4. To listen to families, acknowledge and build upon their strengths and competencies, and learn from families as we support them in their task of nurturing children.

I-2.5. To respect the dignity and preferences of each family and to make an effort to learn about its structure, culture, language, customs, and beliefs.

I-2.6. To acknowledge families' childrearing values and their right to make decisions for their children.

I-2.7. To share information about each child's education and development with families and to help them understand and appreciate the current knowledge base of the early childhood profession.

I-2.8. To help family members enhance their understanding of their children and support the continuing development of their skills as parents.

I-2.9. To participate in building support networks for families by providing them with opportunities to interact with program staff, other families, community resources, and professional services.

Principles

P-2.1. We shall not deny family members access to their child's classroom or program setting unless access is denied by court order or other legal restriction.

P-2.2. We shall inform families of program philosophy, policies, curriculum, assessment system, and personnel qualifications, and explain why we teach as we do—which should be in accordance with our ethical responsibilities to children (see Section I).

P-2.3. We shall inform families of and, when appropriate, involve them in policy decisions.

P-2.4. We shall involve the family in significant decisions affecting their child.

P-2.5. We shall make every effort to communicate effectively with all families in a language that they understand. We shall use community resources for translation and interpretation when we do not have sufficient resources in our own programs.

P-2.6. As families share information with us about their children and families, we shall consider this information to plan and implement the program.

P-2.7. We shall inform families about the nature and purpose of the program's child assessments and how data about their child will be used.

P-2.8. We shall treat child assessment information confidentially and share this information only when there is a legitimate need for it.

P-2.9. We shall inform the family of injuries and incidents involving their child, of risks such as exposures to communicable diseases that might result in infection, and of occurrences that might result in emotional stress.

P-2.10. Families shall be fully informed of any proposed research projects involving their children and shall have the opportunity to give or withhold consent without penalty. We shall not permit or participate in research that could in any way hinder the education, development, or well-being of children.

P-2.11. We shall not engage in or support exploitation of families. We shall not use our relationship with a family for private advantage or personal gain, or enter into relationships with family members that might impair our effectiveness working with their children.

P-2.12. We shall develop written policies for the protection of confidentiality and the disclosure of children's records. These policy documents shall be made available to all program personnel and families. Disclosure of children's records beyond family members, program personnel, and consultants having an obligation of confidentiality shall require familial consent (except in cases of abuse or neglect).

P-2.13. We shall maintain confidentiality and shall respect the family's right to privacy, refraining from disclosure of confidential information and intrusion into family life. However, when we have reason to believe that a child's welfare is at risk, it is permissible to share confidential information with agencies, as well as with individuals who have legal responsibility for intervening in the child's interest.

P-2.14. In cases where family members are in conflict with one another, we shall work openly, sharing our observations of the child, to help all parties involved make informed decisions. We shall refrain from becoming an advocate for one party.

P-2.15. We shall be familiar with and appropriately refer families to community resources and professional support services. After a referral has been made, we shall follow up to ensure that services have been appropriately provided.

Section III. Ethical Responsibilities to Colleagues

In a caring, cooperative workplace, human dignity is respected, professional satisfaction is promoted, and positive relationships are developed and sustained. Based upon our core values, our primary responsibility to colleagues is to establish and maintain settings and relationships that support productive work and meet professional needs. The same ideals that apply to children also apply as we interact with adults in the workplace.

A. Responsibilities to co-workers

Ideals

I-3A.1. To establish and maintain relationships of respect, trust, confidentiality, collaboration, and cooperation with co-workers.

I-3A.2. To share resources with co-workers, collaborating to ensure that the best possible early childhood care and education program is provided.

I-3A.3. To support co-workers in meeting their professional needs and in their professional development.

P-3A.4. To accord co-workers due recognition of professional achievement.

Principles

P-3A.1. We shall recognize the contributions of colleagues to our program and not participate in practices that diminish their reputations or impair their effectiveness in working with children and families.

P-3A.2. When we have concerns about the professional behavior of a co-worker, we shall first let that person know of our concern in a way that shows respect for personal dignity and for the diversity to be found among staff members, and then attempt to resolve the matter collegially and in a confidential manner.

P-3A.3. We shall exercise care in expressing views regarding the personal attributes or professional conduct of co-workers. Statements should be based on firsthand knowledge, not hearsay, and relevant to the interests of children and programs.

P-3A.4. We shall not participate in practices that discriminate against a co-worker because of sex, race, national origin, religious beliefs or other affiliations, age, marital status/family structure, disability, or sexual orientation.

B. Responsibilities to employers

Ideals

I-3B.1. To assist the program in providing the highest quality of service.

I-3B.2. To do nothing that diminishes the reputation of the program in which we work unless it is violating laws and regulations designed to protect children or is violating the provisions of this Code.

Principles

P-3B.1. We shall follow all program policies. When we do not agree with program policies, we shall attempt to effect change through constructive action within the organization.

P-3B.2. We shall speak or act on behalf of an organization only when authorized. We shall take care to acknowledge when we are speaking for the organization and when we are expressing a personal judgment.

P-3B.3. We shall not violate laws or regulations designed to protect children and shall take appropriate action consistent with this Code when aware of such violations.

C. Responsibilities to employees

Ideals

I-3C.1. To promote safe and healthy working conditions and policies that foster mutual respect, cooperation, collaboration, competence, well-being, confidentiality, and self-esteem in staff members.

I-3C.2. To create and maintain a climate of trust and candor that will enable staff to speak and act in the best interests of children, families, and the field of early childhood care and education.

I-3C.3. To strive to secure adequate and equitable compensation (salary and benefits) for those who work with or on behalf of young children.

I-3C.4. To encourage and support continual development of employees in becoming more skilled and knowledgeable practitioners.

Principles

P-3C.1. In decisions concerning children and programs, we shall draw upon the education, training, experience, and expertise of staff members.

P-3C.2. We shall provide staff members with safe and supportive working conditions that honor confidences and permit them to carry out their responsibilities through fair performance evaluation, written grievance procedures, constructive feedback, and opportunities for continuing professional development and advancement.

P-3C.3. We shall develop and maintain comprehensive written personnel policies that define program standards. These policies shall be given to new staff members and shall be available and easily accessible for review by all staff members.

P-3C.4. We shall inform employees whose performance does not meet program expectations of areas of concern and, when possible, assist in improving their performance.

P-3C.5. We shall conduct employee dismissals for just cause, in accordance with all applicable laws and regulations. We shall inform employees who are dismissed of the reasons for their termination. When a dismissal is for cause, justification must be based on evidence of inadequate or inappropriate behavior that is accurately documented, current, and available for the employee to review.

P-3C.6. In making evaluations and recommendations, we shall make judgments based on fact and relevant to the interests of children and programs.

P-3C.7. We shall make hiring, retention, termination, and promotion decisions based solely on a person's competence, record of accomplishment, ability to carry out the responsibilities of the position, and professional preparation specific to the developmental levels of children in his/her care.

P-3C.8. We shall not make hiring, retention, termination, and promotion decisions based on an individual's sex, race, national origin, religious beliefs or other affiliations, age, disability, marital status/family structure, or sexual orientation. We shall be familiar with and observe laws and regulations that pertain to employment discrimination. (Aspects of this principle do not apply to programs that have a lawful mandate to determine eligibility based on one or more of the criteria identified above.)

P-3C.9. We shall maintain confidentiality in dealing with issues related to an employee's job performance and shall respect an employee's right to privacy regarding personal issues.

Section IV. Ethical Responsibilities to Community and Society

Early childhood programs operate within the context of their immediate community made up of families and other institutions concerned with children's welfare. Our responsibilities to the community are to provide programs that meet the diverse needs of families, to cooperate with agencies and professions that share responsibility for children, and to assist families in gaining access to those agencies and allied professionals, and to assist in the development of community programs that are needed but not currently available.

As individuals, we acknowledge our responsibility to provide the best possible programs of care and education for children and to conduct ourselves with honesty and integrity. Because of our specialized expertise in early childhood development and education and because the larger society shares responsibility for the welfare and protection of young children, we acknowledge a collective obligation to advocate for the best interests of children within early childhood programs and in the larger community and to serve as a voice for young children everywhere.

The ideals and principles in this section are presented to distinguish between those that pertain to the work of the individual early childhood educator and those that more typically are engaged in collectively on behalf of the best interests of children—with the understanding that individual early childhood educators have a shared responsibility for addressing the ideals and principles that are identified as "collective."

Ideals (Individual)

I.4.1. To provide the community with high-quality early childhood care and education programs and services.

Ideals (Collective)

I-4.2. To promote cooperation among professionals and agencies and interdisciplinary collaboration among professions concerned with addressing issues in the health, education, and well-being of young children, their families, and early childhood educators.

I-4.3. To work, through education, research, and advocacy toward an environmentally safe world in which all children receive adequate health care, food, and shelter; are nurtured; and live free from violence in their home and their communities.

I-4.4. To work, through education, research, and advocacy toward a society in which all young children have access to high-quality early education and care programs.

I-4.5. To work to ensure that appropriate assessment systems, which include multiple sources of information, are used for purposes that benefit children.

I-4.6. To promote knowledge and understanding of young children and their needs. To work toward greater societal acknowledgment of children's rights and greater social acceptance of responsibility for the well-being of all children.

I-4.7. To support policies and laws that promote the well-being of children and families, and to work to change those that impair their well-being. To participate in developing policies and laws that are needed, and to cooperate with other individuals and groups in these efforts.

I-4.8. To further the professional development of the field of early childhood care and education and to strengthen its commitment to realizing its core values as reflected in this Code.

Principles (Individual)

P-4.1. We shall communicate openly and truthfully about the nature and extent of services that we provide.

P-4.2. We shall apply for, accept, and work in positions for which we are personally well-suited and professionally qualified. We shall not offer services that we do not have the competence, qualifications, or resources to provide.

P-4.3. We shall carefully check references and shall not hire or recommend for employment any person whose competence, qualifications, or character makes him or her unsuited for the position.

P-4.4. We shall be objective and accurate in reporting the knowledge upon which we base our program practices.

P-4.5. We shall be knowledgeable about the appropriate use of assessment strategies and instruments and interpret results accurately to families.

P-4.6. We shall be familiar with laws and regulations that serve to protect the children in our programs and be vigilant in ensuring that these laws and regulations are followed.

P-4.7. When we become aware of a practice or situation that endangers the health, safety, or well-being of children, we have an ethical responsibility to protect children or inform parents and/or others who can.

P-4.8. We shall not participate in practices which are in violation of laws and regulations that protect the children in our programs.

P-4.9. When we have evidence that an early childhood program is violating laws or regulations protecting children, we shall report the violation to appropriate authorities who can be expected to remedy the situation.

P-4.10. When a program violates or requires its employees to violate this Code, it is permissible, after fair assessment of the evidence, to disclose the identity of that program.

Statement of Commitment[4]

As an individual who works with young children, I commit myself to furthering the values of early childhood education as they are reflected in the ideals and principles of the NAEYC Code of Ethical Conduct. To the best of my ability I will:

- Never harm children.
- Ensure that programs for young children are based on current knowledge and research of child development and early childhood education.
- Respect and support families in their task of nurturing children.
- Respect colleagues in early childhood care and education and support them in maintaining the NAEYC Code of Ethical Conduct.
- Serve as an advocate for children, their families, and their teachers in community and society.

[4]This Statement of Commitment is not part of the Code but is a personal acknowledgment of the individual's willingness to embrace the distinctive values and moral obligations of the early childhood care and education. It is recognition of the moral obligations that lead to an individual becoming part of the profession.

- Stay informed of and maintain high standards of professional conduct.
- Engage in an ongoing process of self-reflection, realizing that personal characteristics, biases, and beliefs can have an impact on children and families.

- Be open to new ideas and be willing to learn from the suggestions of others.
- Continue to learn, grow, and contribute as a professional.
- Honor the ideals and principles of the NAEYC Code of Ethical Conduct.

Appendix E

Reasons for Concern That Your Child or a Child in Your Care May Need Special Help

This information may help to relieve or confirm any concerns you may have about a child's development.

Children develop at different rates and in different ways. Differences in development may be related to personality, temperament, and/or experiences. Some children may also have health needs that affect their development.

The first five years are very important in a child's life. The sooner a concern is identified, the sooner a child and family can receive specialized services to support growth and development. Parents, family members, and caregivers may have concerns about a child's development and seek help when needed. It is always a good idea for families to discuss any questions they may have with the child's doctor. Caregivers should discuss concerns with families to see how best to support them.

Risk Factors

The following factors may place children at greater risk for health and developmental concerns:

- Prematurity or low birth weight
- Vision or hearing difficulties
- Prenatal exposure or other types of exposure to drugs, alcohol, or tobacco
- Poor nutrition or difficulties eating (lacks nutritious foods, vitamins, proteins, or iron in diet)
- Exposure to lead-based paint (licking, eating, or sucking on lead-base painted doors, floors, furniture, toys, etc.)
- Environmental factors, such as abuse or neglect

Behaviors and Relationships

Some of the following behaviors may be cause for concern in any child regardless of age:

- Avoids being held, does not like being touched
- Resists being calmed, cannot be comforted
- Avoids or rarely makes eye contact with others
- By age four months, does not coo or smile when interacting with others

Note: The text has been reformatted from the brochure.

- By age one, does not play games such as peek-a-boo or pat-a-cake or wave bye-bye
- By age two, does not imitate parent or caregiver doing everyday things, such as washing dishes, cooking, or brushing teeth
- By age three, does not play with others
- Acts aggressively on a regular basis, hurts self or others

Hearing

- Has frequent earaches
- Has had many ear, nose, or throat infections
- Does not look where sounds or voices are coming from or react to loud noises
- Talks in a very loud or very low voice, or voice has an unusual sound
- Does not always respond when called from across a room even when it is for something that the child is usually interested in or likes
- Turns body so that the same ear is always turned toward a sound

Seeing

- Has reddened, watery eyes or crusty eyelids
- Rubs eyes frequently
- Closes one eye or tilts head when looking at an object
- Has difficulty following objects or looking at people when talked to
- Has difficulty focusing or making eye contact
- Usually holds books or objects very close to face or sits with face very close to television
- Has an eye or eyes that look crossed or turned, or eyes do not move together

Moving

- Has stiff arms or legs
- Pushes away or arches back when held close or cuddled
- By age four months, does not hold head up
- By age six months, does not roll over
- By age one, does not sit up or creep using hands and knees, does not pick up small objects with finger and thumb
- By age two, does not walk alone, has difficulty holding large crayons and scribbling
- By age three, shows poor coordination and falls or stumbles a lot when running, has difficulty turning pages in a book
- By age four, has difficulty standing on one foot for a short time
- By age five, does not skip or hop on one foot, has difficulty drawing simple shapes

Communicating

- By age three months, does not coo or smile
- By age six months, does not babble to get attention
- By age one, does not respond differently to words such as *"night night"* or *"ball"*
- By age one, does not say words to name people or objects, such as *"mama"* or *"bottle,"* or shake head *"no"*
- By age two, does not point to or name objects or people to express wants or needs
- By age two, does not use two-word phrases, such as *"want juice"* or *"mama go"*
- By age three, does not try to say familiar rhymes or songs
- By age three, cannot follow simple directions
- By age four, does not tell stories, whether real or make-believe, or ask questions
- By age four, does not talk so that adults outside the family can understand

Thinking

- By age one, has difficulty finding an object after seeing it hidden
- By age two, does not point to body parts when asked such questions as *"Where's your nose?"*
- By age three, does not play make-believe games
- By age three, does not understand ideas such as *"more"* or *"one"*
- By age four, does not answer simple questions, such as *"What do you do when you are hungry?"* or *"What color is this?"*
- By age five, does not understand the meaning of today, yesterday, or tomorrow

Concerns About a Child's Development

If you have concerns about your child's development, discuss them with your child's doctor. The doctor may recommend calling the local regional center or special education program at either the school district or the county office of education. The family may also contact these agencies directly. If you have concerns about a child in your care, discuss your concerns with the family. This brochure may assist you in talking with the family about specific concerns.

Next Steps

Once contact is made with a regional center or school district, a representative of the agency will provide additional information about services and, if appropriate, make arrangements to have the child assessed. The child may qualify for special services. Parents must give written permission for the child to be assessed and receive special education or early intervention services, which are confidential and provided at no cost to the family. The family may also receive information about local Early Start Family Resource Centers and Family Empowerment Centers on Disability, which provide parent-to-parent support, resource materials, and other information.

Ages Birth to Three Years

Information on local resources regarding birth to three years of age may be obtained from the following agency:

California Department of Developmental Services
P.O. Box 944202, Sacramento, CA 94244-2020
800-515-BABY (2229)
http://www.dds.ca.gov/earlystart
earlystart@dds.ca.gov

Ages Three to Five Years

Information on local resources regarding children three to five years of age may be obtained from the following organizations:

California Department of Education Special Education Division
1430 N Street, Suite 2401, Sacramento, CA 95814
916-445-4613
http://www.cde.ca.gov/sp/se

California Child Care Health Program
1333 Broadway, Suite 1010,
Oakland, CA 94612-1926
Child Care Hotline: 800-333-3212
http://www.ucsfchildcarehealth.org

This brochure is available in English, Spanish, Vietnamese, Hmong, and Chinese.

Ordering information ia available at http://www.cde.ca.gov/re/pn/rc/orderinfo.asp or http://www.wested.org/cs/cpei/print/docs/221

This brochure can be downloaded at http://www.cde.ca.gov/sp/se/fp/concerns.asp or http://www.dds.ca.gov/earlystart

Works Cited

Sources cited in the text appear in this list of references.

Bambini: The Italian Approach to Infant/ Toddler Care. 2001. Edited by L. Gandini and C. Pope Edwards. New York: Teachers College Press.

Barriers to Inclusive Child Care Research Study: Preliminary Findings and Recommendations. 2001. Sacramento: WestEd Center for Prevention and Early Intervention.

Bartlett, A. V.; P. Orton; and M. Turner. 1986. "Day Care Homes: The Silent Majority of Child Day Care," *Review of Infectious Disease*, 8, 663–68.

Bell, D. M., and others. 1989. "Illness Associated with Child Day Care: A Study of Incidence and Cost, *American Journal of Public Health*, 79 (4), 479–84.

Bernhardt, J. L. 2000. "A Primary Caregiving System for Infants and Toddlers: Best for Everyone Involved," *Young Children*, 55 (2), 74–80.

Brault, L. 2003. "Definitions of Developmental Screening, Assessment, and Evaluation." Material generated for inclusion in the *Infant/Toddler Learning and Development Program Guidelines*. Rohnert Park: California Institute of Human Services, Sonoma State University.

Brault, L. M.; J. P. Knapp; and P. J. Winton. 2003. "School Readiness for ALL Children: Ensuring that Children with Disabilities or Other Special Needs are included in California's School Readiness Efforts," in *First 5 School Readiness Initiative Technical Assistance Project*. Los Angeles: UCLA Center for Healthier Children, Families, and Communities.

Bronfenbrenner, U. 1979. *The Ecology of Human Development: Experiments by Nature and Design.* Cambridge, Mass.: Harvard University Press.

Bruner, J. 1983. *Child's Talk.* New York: W. W. Norton & Co.

Bruner, J. 1996. *The Culture of Education.* Cambridge, Mass.: Harvard University Press.

Burchinal, M., and others. 1996. "Quality of Center Child Care and Infant Cognitive and Language Development," *Child Development*, 67 (2): 606–20.

California Child Care Portfolio. 2001. San Francisco: California Child Care Resource and Referral Network.

Caring for Our Children: National Health and Safety Performance Standards Guidelines for Out-of-Home Child Care (Second edition). 2002. Denver: National Resource Center for Health and Safety in Child Care. Available at http://nrc.uchsc.edu/CFOC/index.html.

Carr, A., and M. J. Hanson. 2001. *Positive Outcomes for Children with Disabilities and Other Special Needs: Preliminary Analysis.* Rohnert Park: California Institute of Human Services, Sonoma State University.

Cost, Quality, and Child Outcomes in Child Care Centers. 1995. Edited by S. Helburn. Denver: Economics Department, University of Colorado.

Note: The publication data in this section were supplied by the Child Development Division, California Department of Education. Questions about the references should be directed to the divison at (916) 322-6233.

Derman-Sparks, L. 1995. "Developing Culturally Responsive Caregiving Practices: Acknowledge, Ask, and Adapt," in *Infant/Toddler Caregiving: A Guide to Culturally Sensitive Care.* Developed collaboratively by WestEd and the California Department of Education. Sacramento: California Department of Education, pp. 40–55.

Developmentally Appropriate Practice in Early Childhood Programs Serving Children from Birth Through Age 8: A Position Statement. 1997. Washington, D.C.: National Association for the Education of Young Children.

Discoveries of Infancy: Cognitive Development and Learning. 1992. Child care video and magazine. Sacramento: California Department of Education in collaboration with WestEd Center for Child and Family Studies.

Dombro, A., and L. Wallach. 2001. *The Ordinary Is Extraordinary: How Children Under Three Learn.* N.p.: iUniverse.com.

Ehrle, J.; G. Adams; and K. Tout. 2001. *Who's Caring for Our Youngest Children?* Washington, D.C.: The Urban Institute.

Erickson, M. F., and K. Kurz-Riemer. 1999. *Infants, Toddlers, and Families: A Framework for Support and Intervention.* New York: The Guilford Press.

Fernald, A. 1993. "Human Maternal Vocalizations to Infants as Biologically Relevant Signals: An Evolutionary Perspective," in *Language Acquisition: Core Readings.* Edited by Paul Bloom. Cambridge, Mass.: The MIT Press.

Field, T. M., and others. 1986. "Tactile/Kinesthetic Stimulation Effects on Preterm Neonates," *Pediatrics,* 77, 654–58.

From Neurons to Neighborhoods: The Science of Early Childhood Development. 2000. Edited by J. P. Shonkoff and D. A. Phillips. Washington, D.C.: National Academy Press.

Fuller, B., and S. D. Holloway. 2001. *Preschool and Child-Care Quality in California Neighborhoods: Policy Success, Remaining Gaps.* Berkeley: Policy Analysis for California Education, University of California, Berkeley, and Stanford University and the California Child Care Resource & Referral Network.

Gandini, L., and J. Goldhaber. 2001. "Two Reflections on Documentation: Documentation as a Tool for Promoting the Construction of Respectful Learning," in *Bambini: The Italian Approach to Infant/Toddler Care.* Edited by L. Gandini and C. Pope Edwards. New York: Teachers College Press.

Gardner, J. W. 1996. *Building Community.* Washington, D.C.: Independent Sector.

Gerber, M., and others. 2003. *Dear Parent: Caring for Infants with Respect* (Second edition). Los Angeles: Resources for Infant Educarers (RIE).

Gonzalez-Mena, J. 1997. *Multicultural Issues in Child Care* (Second edition). Mountain View, Calif.: Mayfield Publishing Company.

Gonzalez-Mena, J. 2002. *The Child in the Family and the Community* (Third edition). Upper Saddle River, N.J.: Prentice Hall.

Gopnik, A.; A. N. Meltzoff; and P. K. Kuhl. 2000. *The Scientist in the Crib: What Early Learning Tells Us About the Mind.* New York: HarperCollins.

Greenspan, S. I. 1997. *The Growth of the Mind and the Endangered Origins of Intelligence.* Reading, Mass.: Addison Wesley Longman.

Gunnar, M. 1999. *Studying Stress Physiology in Internationally Adopted Children.* Paper presented at the International Conference on Adoption Research, Minneapolis, Minnesota, August 10–14. Available at http://www.che.umn.edu/fsos/mtarp/incarpapers/gunnar.htm

Hamburg, D. 1996. Foreword to R. Shore, *Family Support and Parent Education: Opportunities for Scaling Up.* New York: Carnegie Corporation.

Hardy, A. M., and M. G. Fowler. 1993. "Child Care Arrangements and Repeated Ear Infections in Young Children," *American Journal of Public Health*, 83 (9), 1321–25.

Hart, B., and T. Risley. 1995. "The Importance of the First Three Years of Family Experience," in *Meaningful Differences in the Everyday Experience of Young American Children*. Baltimore, Md.: Paul H. Brookes Publishing. pp. 175–189.

Hart, B., and T. Risley. 2003. "The Early Catastrophe: The 30 Million Word Gap," *American Educator* (Spring), 27(1), 4–9.

Heckman, J. J. 2000. *Policies to Foster Human Capital*. Chicago: University of Chicago Department of Economics.

Herschkowitz, N., and E. C. Herschkowitz. 2002. *A Good Start in Life: Understanding Your Child's Brain and Behavior*. Washington, D.C.: Joseph Henry Press.

How People Learn: Brain, Mind, Experience, and School. 1999. Edited by J. D. Bransford, A. L. Brown, and R. R. Cocking. Washington, D.C.: National Academy Press.

Howes, C. 1997. "Children's Experiences in Center-Based Child Care as a Function of Teacher Background and Adult:Child Ratio," *Merrill-Palmer Quarterly*, 43 (3), 404–25.

Howes, C. 1999. "Attachment Relationships in the Context of Multiple Caregivers," in *Attachment Theory, Research, and Clinical Applications*. Edited by J. Cassidy and P. R. Shaver. New York: The Guilford Press.

Howes, C. 2000. "Social–Emotional Classroom Climate in Child Care, Child-Teacher Relationships and Children's Second Grade Peer Relations," *Social Development*, 9 (2), 191–205.

Improving Schooling for Language-Minority Children: A Research Agenda. 1997. Edited by D. August and K. Hakuta. Washington, D.C.: National Academy Press.

Infant/Toddler Caregiving: A Guide to Setting Up Environments. 1990. Developed by WestEd. Sacramento: California Department of Education.

Kagan, S. L., and N. E. Cohen. 1997. *Not by Chance: A Vision for America's Early Care and Education System*. Final Report of the Quality 2000 Initiative. New Haven, Conn.: Yale University.

Kuhl, P. K. 2000. "A New View of Language Acquisition," *Proceedings of the National Academy of Sciences*, 97 (22), 11850–57.

Kuhn, C. M., and others. 1991. "Tactile-Kinesthetic Stimulation Effects on Sympathetic and Adrenocortical Function in Preterm Infants," *Journal of Pediatrics*, 119, 434–40.

Lally, J. R., and others. 1995. *Caring for Infants and Toddlers in Groups: Developmentally Appropriate Practice*. Washington, D.C.: Zero to Three.

Map to Inclusive Child Care Project: Access to Child Care for Children with Disabilities and Other Special Needs. 2001. Sacramento: California Department of Education, Child Development Division.

NAEYC Code of Ethical Conduct and Statement of Commitment. 2005. Washington, D.C.: National Association for the Education of Young Children (brochure).

National Institute of Child Health and Development (NICHD) Early Child Care Research Network. "The Relation of Child Care to Cognitive and Language Development." 2000. *Child Development*, 71 (4), 960–80.

Ordóñez, C., and others. 2002. "Depth and Breadth of Vocabulary in Two Languages: Which Vocabulary Skills Transfer?" *Journal of Educational Psychology*, 94 (4), 719–28.

Parlakian, R., and N. Seibel. 2001. *Being in Charge: Reflective Leadership in Infant/Family Programs*. Washington, D.C.: Zero to Three Center for Program Excellence.

Pawl, J. H. 1990a. "Infants in Day Care: Reflections on Experiences, Expectations and Relationships," *Zero to Three* (February), 10 (3).

Pawl, J. H. 1990b. "Self-esteem, Security, and Social Competence: Ten Caregiving Gifts, in *Infant/Toddler Caregiving: A Guide to Social–Emotional Growth and Socialization*. Developed by WestEd. Sacramento: California Department of Education.

Peisner-Feinberg, E. S., and others. 1999. *The Children of the Cost, Quality, and Outcomes Study Go to School*. Chapel Hill: University of North Carolina, Frank Porter Graham Child Development Center.

Perry, B. D. 1996. Click on "Keep the Cool in School." Available online at http://www.teacher.scholastic.com/professional/bruceperry/index.htm.

Pope E. C., and H. Raikes. 2002. "Extending the Dance: Relationship-Based Approaches to Infant/Toddler Care and Education," *Young Children,* 57 (4), 10–17.

Presler, B. 1996. *Health and Safety Considerations: Caring for Young Children with Exceptional Health Care Needs*. Rohnert Park: Sonoma State University, California Institute of Human Services.

Ramey, C., and S. L. Ramey. 1999. *Right from Birth: Building Your Child's Foundation for Life*. New York: Goddard Press.

Reasons for Concern That Your Child or a Child in Your Care May Need Special Help. 2004. Sacramento: California Department of Education in collaboration with the California Department of Developmental Services (brochure).

Regional Educational Laboratories Early Childhood Collaboration Network. 1995. *Continuity in Early Childhood: A Framework for Home, School, and Community Linkages*. Oak Brook, Ill.: Author.

"The Relationship of Child Care to Cognitive and Language Development." 1997. NICHD Study of Early Child Care. Paper presented at the Society for Research in Child Development meeting, Washington, D.C., April 3–6.

Rinaldi, C. 2001. "Reggio Emilia: The Image of the Child and the Child's Environment as a Fundamental Principle," in *Bambini: The Italian Approach to Infant/Toddler Care*. Edited by L. Gandini and C. P. Edwards. New York: Teachers College Press, pp. 49–54.

Rinaldi, C. 2003. "The Image of the Child." Lecture given to Reggio Emilia Study Group Tour, Reggio Emilia, Italy, April 8.

Schore, A. N. 1994. *Affect Regulation and the Origin of the Self: The Neurobiology of Emotional Development*. Hillsdale, N.J.: Lawrence Erlbaum Associates.

Shore, R. 1997. *Rethinking the Brain: New Insights into Early Development*. New York: Families and Work Institute.

Shore, R. 2002. *What Kids Need: Today's Best Ideas for Nurturing, Teaching, and Protecting Young Children*. Boston: Beacon Press.

Siegel A. C., and R. V. Burton. 1999. "Effects of Baby Walkers on Motor and Mental Development in Human Infants," *Journal of Developmental and Behavioral Pediatrics* (October), 20 (5), 355–61.

Snyder, K., and G. Adams. 2001. *State Child Care Profile for Children with Employed Mothers: California*. Assessing the New Federalism. Washington, D.C.: The Urban Institute.

Sroufe, L. A. 1995. *Emotional Development: The Organization of Emotional Life in the Early Years*. New York: Cambridge University Press.

Starting Out Right: A Guide to Promoting Children's Reading Success. 1999. Edited by M. S. Burns, P. Griffin, and C. E. Snow. Washington, D.C.: National Academy Press.

Thomas, A., and S. Chess. 1977. *Temperament and Development.* New York: Bunner/Mazel.

Together in Care: Meeting the Intimacy Needs of Infants and Toddlers in Groups. 1992. San Francisco: Far West Laboratory (video magazine).

Torelli, L. 2002. "Enhancing Development Through Classroom Design in Early Head Start," *Children and Families* (Spring), 16 (2), 44–51.

Torelli, L., and C. Durrett. 1998. *Landscapes for Learning: Designing Group Care Environments for Infants and Toddlers.* Berkeley: Torelli/Durrett Infant and Toddler Child Care Furniture.

Whitebook, M.; L. Sakai; E. Gerber; and C. Howes. 2001. *Then and Now: Changes in Child Care Staffing, 1994–2000.* Washington D.C.: Center for the Child Care Workforce.

Who Cares for America's Children? Child Care Policy for the 1990s. 1990. Edited by C. D. Hayes, J. L. Palmer, and M. J. Zaslow. Washington, D.C.: National Academy Press.

Williams, L. R., and Y. De Gaetano. 1985. *Alerta : A Multicultural, Bilingual Approach to Teaching Young Children.* Menlo Park: Addison-Wesley Pub. Co.

Williamson, G. G., and M. E. Anzalone. 2001. *Sensory Integration and Self-Regulation in Infants and Toddlers: Helping Very Young Children Interact with Their Environment.* Washington, D.C.: Zero to Three.

Further Reading

Ada, A. F., and C. Baker. 2001. *Guía Para Padres y Maestros de Niños Bilingües.* Clevedon UK: Multilingual Matters.

African American Early Childhood Resource Center. 1998. *Resources to Build Diverse Leadership.* Washington, D.C.: National Black Child Development Institute.

Bailey, D. B., and M. Wolery. 1992. *Teaching Infants and Preschoolers with Disabilities.* Englewood Cliffs, N.J.: Prentice Hall.

Baker, C. 1995. *A Parents' and Teachers' Guide to Bilingualism.* Clevedon UK: Multilingual Matters.

Barrera, I., and R. M. Corso. 2003. *Skilled Dialogue.* Baltimore, Md.: Paul H. Brookes Publishing.

Bergen, D.; R. Reid; and L. Torelli. 2001. *Educating and Caring for Very Young Children: The Infant/Toddler Curriculum.* New York: Teachers College Press.

Bertacchi, J. 1996. "Relationship-Based Organizations," *Zero to Three,* 17 (2), 1, 3–7.

Bondurant-Utz, J. A. 1994. "Cultural Diversity," in *A Practical Guide to Infant and Preschool Assessment in Special Education.* Edited by J. A. Bondurant-Utz and L. B. Luciano. Needham Heights, Mass.: Allyn and Bacon.

Brazelton, T. B., and S. I. Greenspan. 2000. *The Irreducible Needs of Children: What Every Child Must Have to Grow, Learn, and Flourish.* Cambridge, Mass.: Perseus Publishing.

Burton, A., and M. Whitebook. 1998. *Child Care Staff Compensation Guidelines for California 1998.* Washington, D.C.: Center for the Child Care Workforce. (Prepared for the California Department of Education.)

Campbell, F. A., and C. Ramey. 1999. *Early Learning, Later Success: The Abecedarian Study.* Chapel Hill, N.C.: University of North Carolina, Frank Porter Graham Child Development Center.

The Child Development Associate Assessment System and Competency Standards: Infant/ Toddler Caregivers in Center-Based Programs. 1999. Washington, D.C.: The Council for Professional Recognition.

Comer, J. P., and A. F. Poussaint. 1992. *Raising Black Children: Two Leading Psychiatrists Confront the Educational, Social, and Emotional Problems Facing Black Children.* New York: Plume Books.

Cunningham, B., and L. W. Watson. 2002. "Recruiting Male Teachers," *Young Children* (November), 10–15.

Dombro, A. L., and P. Bryan. 1991. *Sharing the Caring: How to Find the Right Child Care and Make It Work for You and Your Child.* New York: Simon and Schuster.

Eliot, L. 1999. *What's Going on in There?* New York: Bantam Books.

Fostering the Development of a First and a Second Language in Early Childhood: Resource Guide. 1998. Sacramento: California Department of Education.

The Future of Children: Caring for Infants and Toddlers. 2001. (Spring/Summer) 2 (1). Los Altos: The David and Lucile Packard Foundation.

Galinsky, E.; C. Howes; and S. Kontos. 1995. *The Family Child Care Training Study.* New York: Families and Work Institute.

Geary, D. C., and M. V. Finn. 2001. "Evolution of Human Parental Behavior and the Human Family," *Parenting Science and Practice* (January-June), 1 (1-2), 5–41.

Gerber, M., and others. 2003. *Dear Parent: Caring for Infants with Respect.* Edited by Joan Weaver. Los Angeles: Resources for Infant Educarers.

Golinkoff, R. M., and K. Hirsh-Pasek. 1999. *How Babies Talk: The Magic and Mystery of Language in the First Three Years.* New York: Plume Penguin Group.

Gonzalez-Mena, J. 1992. "Taking a Culturally Sensitive Approach in Infant-Toddler Programs," *Young Children* (January), 47 (2), 4–9.

Gonzalez-Mena, J. 2001. *The Child in the Family and Community* (Third edition). Upper Saddle River, N.J.: Prentice Hall.

Gonzalez-Mena, J. 2001. *Multicultural Issues in Child Care* (Third edition). Mountain View, Calif.: Mayfield Publishing Company.

Gonzalez-Mena, J., and D. Widmeyer Eyer. 2001. *Infants, Toddlers, and Caregivers* (Fifth edition). Mountain View, Calif.: Mayfield Publishing Company.

Greenspan, S. 1999. *Building Healthy Minds.* Cambridge, Mass.: Perseus Books.

Harms, T.; R. M. Clifford; and D. Cryer. 1998. *Early Childhood Environment Rating Scale* (Revised edition). New York: Teachers College Press.

Helburn, S. W., and C. Howes. 1996. "Child Care Cost and Quality," *The Future of Children,* 6 (2), 62–72.

Hofferth, S. 1999. "Child Care, Maternal Employment, and Public Policy," in *The Silent Crisis in U.S. Child Care.* Edited by S. W. Helburn. Philadelphia: American Academy of Political and Social Science (May), 563, 20–38.

Holloway, S. D., and others. 1997. *Through My Own Eyes: Single Mothers and the Cultures of Poverty.* Cambridge, Mass.: Harvard University Press.

Howes, C., and C. E. Hamilton. 1993. "Child Care for Young Children," in *Handbook of Research on the Education of Young Children.* Edited by B. Spodek. New York: Macmillan, pp. 322–36.

Infant/Toddler Caregiving: A Guide to Culturally Sensitive Care. 1995. Developed by WestEd. The Program for Infant/Toddler Caregivers. Sacramento: California Department of Education.

Jablon, J. R.; A. L. Dombro; and M. L. Dichtelmiller. 1999. *The Power of Observation.* Washington, D.C.: Teaching Strategies, Inc.

Karr-Morse, R., and M. S. Wiley. 1999. *Ghosts from the Nursery: Tracing the Roots of Violence.* New York: The Atlantic Monthly Press.

Kim, U., and S. Choi. 1994. "Individualism, Collectivism, and Child Development: A Korean Perspective," in *The Cross-Cultural Roots of Minority Child Development.* Edited by P. M. Greenfield and R. R. Cocking. Hillsdale, N.J.: Erlbaum, pp. 227–57.

Kontos, S., and others. 1994. *Quality in Family Child Care and Relative Care.* New York: Teachers College Press.

Lally, J. R. 1997. "Brain Development in Infancy: A Critical Period," *Bridges,* 3 (1).

Lally, J. R., A. Griffin; E. Fenichel; M. Segal; E. Szanton; and B. Weissbourd. 1995. *Caring for Infants and Toddlers in Groups: Developmentally Appropriate Practice.* Washington, D.C.: Zero to Three.

Lally, J. R.; P. L. Mangione; and A. Honig. 1988. "The Syracuse University Family Development Research Program: Long-Range Impact of an Early Intervention with Low-Income Children and Their Families," in *Parent Education in Early Childhood Intervention: Emerging Directions in Theory, Research, and Practice,* Vol. 3. Edited by D. R. Powell and I. E. Sigel. Norwood, N.J.: Ablex.

Lally, J. R.; Y. L. Torres; and P. C. Phelps. 1994. "Caring for Infants and Toddlers in Groups: Necessary Considerations for Emotional, Social, and Cognitive Development," *Zero to Three*, 14 (5), 1–8.

Langone, J.; D. M. Malone; and T. Kinsley. 1999. "Technology Solutions for Young Children with Developmental Concerns," *Infants and Young Children* (April), 65–76.

Learning Through Supervision and Mentorship to Support the Development of Infants, Toddlers and Their Families: A Source Book. 1992. Edited by E. Fenichel. Washington, D.C.: Zero to Three.

Leavitt, R. L. 1994. *Power and Emotion in Infant-Toddler Day Care.* Edited by M. A. Jensen. Albany, N.Y.: State University of New York Press.

Lieberman, A. F. 1993. *The Emotional Life of the Toddler.* New York: The Free Press.

Lombardi, J., and J. Poppe. 2001. "Investing in Better Care for Infants and Toddlers: The Next Frontier for School Readiness," *NCSL State Legislative Report* (October), 26 (10), 1.

"Map to Services for Children with Special Needs and Their Families." 1999. *Bridges,* 4 (1), 20–21.

National Institute of Child Health and Development (NICHD) Early Child Care Research Network. "Child Care Structure, Process, Outcome: Direct and Indirect Effects of Child Care Quality on Young Children's Development." 2002. *Psychological Science* (May) 13 (3), 199–206.

National Institute of Child Health and Development (NICHD) Early Child Care Research Network. "Child Outcomes When Child Care Center Classes Meet Recommended Standards for Quality." 1999. *American Journal of Public Health* (July), 89 (7), 1072–77.

Parlakian, R. 2001. *Look, Listen, and Learn: Reflective Supervision and Relationship-Based Work.* Washington, D.C.: Zero to Three.

Parlakian, R., and N. L. Siebel. 2001. *Being in Charge: Reflective Leadership in Infant/ Family Programs.* Washington, D.C.: Zero to Three.

Parlakian, R., and N. L. Siebel. 2002. *Building Strong Foundations: Practical Guidance for Promoting the Social Development of Infants and Toddlers.* Washington, D.C.: Zero to Three.

Pawl, J. H., and A. L. Dombro. 2001. *Learning and Growing Together with Families: Partnering with Parents to Support Young Children's Development.* Washington, D.C.: Zero to Three.

Peisner-Feinberg, E. S., and others. 1999a. *The Children of the Cost, Quality, and Outcomes Study Go to School.* Executive Summary. Chapel Hill: University of North Carolina, Chapel Hill.

Peisner-Feinberg, E. S., and others. 1999b. *The Children of the Cost, Quality, and Outcomes Study Go to School.* Technical Report. Raleigh, N.C.: National Center for Early Development and Learning, University of North Carolina, Chapel Hill.

Phillips, D. A.; K. McCartney; and S. Scarr. 1987. "Child-Care Quality and Children's Social Development," *Developmental Psychology*, 23, 537–43.

Pica, R. 1996. "Beyond Physical Development: Why Young Children Need to Move," *Young Children* (September), 4–11.

Plomin, R., and J. C. DeFries. 1998. "The Genetics of Cognitive Abilities and Disabilities," *Scientific American* (May), 62–69.

Purves, D., and J. W. Lichtman. 1985. *Principles of Neural Development.* Sunderland, Mass.: Sinauer Associates, Inc.

Reflective Supervision in Practice: Stories from the Field. 2002. Edited by R. Parlakian. Washington, D.C.: Zero to Three.

Rogoff, B. 1990. *Apprenticeship in Thinking: Cognitive Development in Social Context.* New York and Oxford: Oxford University Press.

Rose, S. A.; J. F. Feldman; and J. J. Jankowski. 2002. "Processing Speed in the First Year of Life: A Longitudinal Study of Preterm and Full-Term Infants," *Developmental Psychology*, 38 (6), 895–902.

Schurch, P. 1990. "A Multicultural Perspective on Programming for Toddlers," in *Trusting Toddlers: Planning for One- to Three-Year-Olds in Child Care Centers*. Edited by A. Stonehouse. St. Paul, Minn.: Redleaf Press.

Segal, M. 1998. *Your Child at Play: Birth to One Year* (Second edition). New York: Newmarket Press.

Siegel, D. J. 1999. *The Developing Mind: Toward a Neurobiology of Interpersonal Experience*. New York: Guilford Press.

Torelli, L. 2002. "Enhancing Development through Classroom Design in Early Head Start," *Children and Families* (Spring), 16 (2).

Vygotsky, L. 1978. *Mind in Society: The Development of Higher Psychological Processes*. Cambridge, Mass.: Harvard University Press.

Who Cares for America's Children: Child Care Policy for the 1990s. 1990. Edited by S. Hayes, F. Palmer, and M. Zaslow. Washington, D.C.: National Academy Press.

Whitebook, M., and D. Bellm. 1999. *Taking on Turnover: An Action Guide for Child Care Center Teachers and Directors*. Washington, D.C.: Center for the Child Care Workforce.

Whitebook, M., and others. 1996. *California Child Care and Development and Compensation Study: Towards Promising Policy and Practice*. Washington, D.C.: National Center for the Early Childhood Work Force. Palo Alto, Calif.: American Institutes for Research.

Whitebook, M.; C. Howes; and D. Phillips. 1990. *Who Cares? Child Care Teachers and the Quality of Care in America*. Final Report of the National Child Care Staffing Study. Oakland, Calif.: Child Care Employee Project.

Williams, L. R., and Y. De Gaetano (contributor). 1985. *Alerta: A Multicultural, Bilingual Approach to Teaching Young Children*. Menlo Park, Calif.: Addison-Wesley Publishing Company.

Williamson, G., and M. Anzalone. 2001. *Sensory Integration and Self-Regulation in Infants and Toddlers*. Washington, D.C.: Zero to Three.

Zigler, E.; M. Finn-Stevenson; and N. Hall. 2003. *The First Three Years and Beyond: Brain Development and Social Policy*. New Haven, Conn.: Yale University Press.

Program for Infant toddler care

Price List and Order Form

MODULE I

Social–Emotional Growth and Socialization

DVDs/Videos and Magazines

First Moves: Welcoming a Child to a New Caregiving Setting

Flexible, Fearful, or Feisty: The Different Temperaments of Infants and Toddlers

Getting in Tune: Creating Nurturing Relationships with Infants and Toddlers

Print Materials

Infant/Toddler Caregiving: A Guide to Social–Emotional Growth and Socialization

Module I Trainer's Manual

MODULE II

Group Care

DVDs/Videos and Magazines

It's Not Just Routine: Feeding, Diapering, and Napping Infants and Toddlers (Second edition)

Respectfully Yours: Magda Gerber's Approach to Professional Infant/ Toddler Care

Space to Grow: Creating a Child Care Environment for Infants and Toddlers (Second edition)

Together in Care: Meeting the Intimacy Needs of Infants and Toddlers in Groups

Print Materials

Infant/Toddler Caregiving: A Guide to Routines (Second edition)

Infant/Toddler Caregiving: A Guide to Setting Up Environments

Module II Trainer's Manual

MODULE III

Learning and Development

DVDs/Videos and Magazines

The Ages of Infancy: Caring for Young, Mobile, and Older Infants

Discoveries of Infancy: Cognitive Development and Learning

Early Messages: Facilitating Language Development and Communication

The Next Step: Including the Infant in the Curriculum

Print Materials

Infant/Toddler Caregiving: A Guide to Cognitive Development and Learning

Infant/Toddler Caregiving: A Guide to Language Development and Communication

Module III Trainer's Manual

MODULE IV

Culture, Family, and Providers

DVDs/Videos and Magazines

Essential Connections: Ten Keys to Culturally Sensitive Child Care

Protective Urges: Working with the Feelings of Parents and Caregivers

Print Materials

Infant/Toddler Caregiving: A Guide to Creating Partnerships with Families

Infant/Toddler Caregiving: A Guide to Culturally Sensitive Care

Module IV Trainer's Manual

Each module includes DVDs or videos, video magazines, and curriculum guide(s), all available in English and Spanish, and a trainer's manual. Most videos are also available in Chinese (Cantonese). Additional PITC materials and new infant/toddler items from the California Department of Education are listed on the last page of this order form.

Module I: Social–Emotional Growth and Socialization

Title	Item no.	Quantity	Price	Total
Audiovisual Materials				
DVD (Each DVD includes a video magazine in the same language as the DVD.)				
First Moves (1988)	1636		$75.00	
Los primeros pasos (1988)	1637		75.00	
Flexible, Fearful, or Feisty (1990)	1638		75.00	
Flexible, cauteloso, o inquieto (1990)	1639		75.00	
Getting in Tune (1990)	1644		75.00	
Llevar el compás (1990)	1645		75.00	
VHS (Each video includes a video magazine in English.)				
First Moves - English (1988)	0751		$75.00	
First Moves - Spanish (1988)	0771		75.00	
First Moves - Chinese (Cantonese) (1988)	0772		75.00	
First Moves - PAL English (1988)	1416		75.00	
Flexible, Fearful, or Feisty - English (1990)	0839		75.00	
Flexible, Fearful, or Feisty - Spanish (1990)	0872		75.00	
Flexible, Fearful, or Feisty - Chinese (Cantonese) (1990)	0871		75.00	
Flexible, Fearful, or Feisty - PAL English (1990)	1417		75.00	
Getting in Tune - English (1990)	0809		75.00	
Getting in Tune - Spanish (1990)	0811		75.00	
Getting in Tune - Chinese (Cantonese) (1990)	0810		75.00	
Getting in Tune - PAL English (1990)	1418		75.00	
Print Materials				
Curriculum Guides				
A Guide to Social–Emotional Growth and Socialization (1990)	0876		$18.00	
Una guía para el crecimiento socioemocional y la socialización (2005)	1606		18.00	
Module I Trainer's Manual (1993)	1084		25.00	
Video Magazines (In packages of 50)				
First Moves - English	9960		$23.00	
First Moves - Spanish	9736		23.00	
Flexible, Fearful, or Feisty - English	9956		23.00	
Flexible, Fearful, or Feisty - Spanish	9737		23.00	
Getting in Tune - English	9957		23.00	
Getting in Tune - Spanish	9738		23.00	

Module I: Social–Emotional Growth and Socialization Package—$239
Price includes 3 videos, 3 accompanying video magazines, 1 curriculum guide, and 1 trainer's manual.

Title	Item no.	Quantity	Price	Total
English videos/English guides/English manual	9928		**$239.00**	
English DVDs/English guides/English manual	9696		**239.00**	
Spanish videos/Spanish guides/English manual	9929		**239.00**	
Spanish DVDs/Spanish guides/English manual	9695		**239.00**	
Chinese (Cantonese) videos/English guides/English manual	9930		**239.00**	
PAL English videos/English guides/English manual	9728		**239.00**	

Module II: Group Care

Title	Item no.	Quantity	Price	Total
Audiovisual Materials				
DVD (Each DVD includes a video magazine in the same language as the DVD.)				
It's Not Just Routine (Second edition) (2000)	1648		$75.00	
No es sólo una rutina (Segunda edición) (2000)	1649		75.00	
Respectfully Yours (1988)	1640		75.00	
Con respeto (1988)	1641		75.00	
Space to Grow (Second edition) (2004)	1646		75.00	
Un lugar para crecer (Segunda edición) (2004)	1647		75.00	
Together in Care (1992)	1632		75.00	
Unidos en el corazón (1992)	1633		75.00	
VHS (Each video includes a video magazine in English.)				
It's Not Just Routine - (Second edition) English (2000)	1483		$75.00	
It's Not Just Routine - (Second edition) Spanish (2000)	1484		75.00	
It's Not Just Routine - (Second edition) Chinese (Cantonese) (2000)	1485		75.00	
It's Not Just Routine - (Second edition) PAL English (2000)	1506		75.00	
Respectfully Yours - English (1988)	0753		75.00	
Respectfully Yours - Spanish (1988)	0773		75.00	
Respectfully Yours - Chinese (Cantonese) (1988)	0774		75.00	
Respectfully Yours - PAL English (1988)	1422		75.00	
Space to Grow - (Second edition) English (2004)	1595		75.00	
Space to Grow - (Second edition) Spanish (2004)	1596		75.00	
Space to Grow - PAL English (2004)	1423		75.00	
Together in Care - English (1992)	1044		75.00	
Together in Care - Spanish (1992)	0888		75.00	
Together in Care - Chinese (Cantonese) (1992)	1051		75.00	
Together In Care - PAL English (1992)	1424		75.00	
Print Materials				
Curriculum Guides				
A Guide to Routines (Second edition) (2000)	1510		$18.00	
Una guía para las rutinas cotidianas del cuidado infantil (Segunda edición) (2004)	1602		18.00	
A Guide to Setting Up Environments (1990)	0879		18.00	
Una guía para crear los ambientes del cuidado infantil (2006)	1614		18.00	
Modulo II Trainer's Manual (1993)	1076		25.00	
Video Magazines (In packages of 50)				
It's Not Just Routine (Second edition) - English	9724		$23.00	
It's Not Just Routine (Second edition) - Spanish	9723		23.00	
Respectfully Yours - English	9958		23.00	
Respectfully Yours - Spanish	9740		23.00	
Space to Grow (Second edition) - English	9709		23.00	
Space to Grow (Second edition) - Spanish	9710		23.00	
Together in Care - English	9873		23.00	
Together in Care - Spanish	9742		23.00	

Module II: Group Care Package—$319

Price includes 4 videos, 4 accompanying video magazines, 2 curriculum guides, and 1 trainer's manual.

English videos/English guides/English manual	9931		**$319.00**	
English DVDs/English guides/English manual	9694		**319.00**	
Spanish videos/Spanish guides/English manual	9932		**319.00**	
Spanish DVDs/Spanish guides/English manual	9693		**319.00**	
Chinese (Cantonese) videos/English guides/English manual (Does not include Space to Grow video)	9933		**249.00**	
PAL English videos/English guides/English manual	9729		**319.00**	

Module III: Learning and Development

Title	Item no.	Quantity	Price	Total
Audiovisual Materials				
DVD (Each DVD includes a video magazine in the same language as the DVD.)				
The Ages of Infancy (1990)	1634		$75.00	
Las edades de la infancia (1990)	1635		75.00	
Discoveries of Infancy (1992)	1623		75.00	
Descubrimientos de la infancia (1992)	1624		75.00	
Early Messages (1998)	1625		75.00	
El comenzar de la communicación (1998)	1626		75.00	
The Next Step (2004)	1621		75.00	
El siguiente paso (2004)	1622		75.00	
VHS (Each video includes a video magazine in English.)				
The Ages of Infancy - English (1990)	0883		$75.00	
The Ages of Infancy - Spanish (1990)	0884		75.00	
The Ages of Infancy - Chinese (Cantonese) (1990)	0885		75.00	
The Ages of Infancy - PAL English (1990)	1413		75.00	
Discoveries of Infancy - English (1992)	1045		75.00	
Discoveries of Infancy - Spanish (1992)	0829		75.00	
Discoveries of Infancy - Chinese (Cantonese) (1992)	0784		75.00	
Discoveries of Infancy - PAL English (1992)	1414		75.00	
Early Messages - English (1998)	1425		75.00	
Early Messages - Spanish (1998)	1446		75.00	
Early Messages - Chinese (Cantonese) (1998)	1447		75.00	
Early Messages - PAL English (1998)	1426		75.00	
The Next Step - English (2004)	1554		75.00	
The Next Step - Spanish (2004)	1593		75.00	
Print Materials				
Curriculum Guides				
A Guide to Cognitive Development and Learning (1995)	1055		$18.00	
Una guía para el desarrollo cognitivo y el aprendizaje (2006)	1616		18.00	
A Guide to Language Development and Communication (1990)	0880		18.00	
Una guía para el desarrollo del lenguaje y la comunicación (2006)	1608		18.00	
Module III Trainer's Manual (1993)	1108		25.00	
Video Magazines (In packages of 50)				
The Ages of Infancy - English	9954		$23.00	
The Ages of Infancy - Spanish	9732		23.00	
Discoveries of Infancy - English	9874		23.00	
Discoveries of Infancy - Spanish	9733		23.00	
Early Messages - English	9747		23.00	
Early Messages - Spanish	9734		23.00	
The Next Step - English	9715		23.00	
The Next Step - Spanish	9697		23.00	

Module III: Learning and Development Package—$249

Price includes 4 videos, 4 accompanying video magazines, 2 curriculum guides, and 1 trainer's manual.

English videos/English guides/English manual	9860		**$249.00**	
English DVDs/English guides/English manual	9692		**249.00**	
Spanish videos/Spanish guides/English manual	9861		**249.00**	
Spanish DVDs/Spanish guides/English manual	9691		**249.00**	
Chinese (Cantonese) videos/English guides/English manual	9862		**249.00**	
PAL English videos/English guides/English manual	9730		**249.00**	